T3-BPE-230

MARKETING INVESTMENT MANAGEMENT SERVICES

INNOVATIVE
STRATEGIES
FOR▶
CAPTURING
AND▶
KEEPING
▲KEY
INSTITUTIONAL
ACCOUNTS

EDITORS

● N I C K
MENCHER
●BRIAN R.
B R U C E

PROBUS PUBLISHING COMPANY
Chicago, Illinois
Cambridge, England

332.6
M345

© 1992, Nick Mencher and Brian R. Bruce

ALL RIGHTS RESERVED. No part of this publication may be repro-
duced, stored in a retrieval systems, or transmitted, in any form or
by any means, electronic, mechanical, photocopying, recording, or
otherwise, without the prior written permission of the publisher and
the copyright holder.

This publication is designed to provide accurate and authoritative
information in regard to the subject matter covered. It is sold with
the understanding that the publisher is not engaged in rendering
legal, accounting, or other professional service.

Authorization to photocopy items for internal or personal use, or the
internal or personal use of specific clients, is granted by PROBUS
PUBLISHING COMPANY, provided that the U.S. $7.00 per page fee
is paid directly to Copyright Clearance Center, 27 Congress Street,
Salem, MA 01970, USA. For those organizations that have been
granted a photocopy license by CCC, a separate system of payment
has been arranged. The fee code for users of the Transactional
Reporting Service is 1-55738-261-1/92/$00.00 + $7.00.

ISBN 1-55738-261-1

Printed in the United States of America

BB

1 2 3 4 5 6 7 8 9 0
TP

CONTENTS

UNIVERSITY LIBRARIES
CARNEGIE-MELLON UNIVERSITY
PITTSBURGH, PENNSYLVANIA 15213

II / The Marketing Process: Preparing to Win

THE AUTHORS

BRIAN R. BRUCE

Vice President
State Street Bank and Trust

Mr. Bruce is a Vice President and Unit Head in the Asset Management Area of State Street Bank and Trust Company in Boston, Mass. His responsibilities include portfolio management, currency hedging, and research and development. He is currently Editor of a new journal published by Institutional Investor and has authored and edited several other books on investing including *Real Estate Portfolio Management* (Probus 1991) *and Quantitative International Investing* (Probus 1990).

Mr. Bruce received an M.S. in Computer Science from DePaul University and an M.B.A. in Finance from the University of Chicago, where he won the prestigious CEO Award.

JACQUELINE L. CHARNLEY

Chairman of the Board
Charnley & Røstvold, Inc.

In 1978, Ms. Charnley co-established Charnley & Røstvold, Inc., to help investment management organizations with their marketing, sales, and communication programs to tax-exempt prospects and clients.

IIer firm analyzes the competitive strengths and weaknesses of investment organizations, provides rankings against manager selection criteria, designs verbal and written presentations, writes support material, conducts industry-related research, and holds workshops on these various topics.

Prior to forming Charnley & Røstvold, Ms. Charnley worked with Collins Associates as an investment manager research analyst. She was involved with corporate client programs, traveling with pension committees on manager searches, attending initial prospect and final presentations, and organizing client quarterly meetings.

Ms. Charnley received her bachelor's degree in English from the University of California at Irvine.

DANA DAKIN

President
Dakin & Willison

Ms. Dakin founded Dana Dakin Associates (now Dakin & Willison) in 1976 to provide communications and marketing consulting services to the institutional investment field.

Prior to establishing Dana Dakin Associates, she was an Assistant Vice President with Callan Associates. As manager of Callan's technical staff, she was responsible for overseeing performance measurement, portfolio audits, analysis for manager searches and client reporting.

Ms. Dakin has addressed the Institutional Investor Marketing Roundtable, and is a frequent speaker at investment industry conferences. Under her creative direction, Dakin & Willison has won numerous communications awards, including the New York Art Directors Award, the Desi and the STA 100.

She is a graduate of Scripps College (International Relations), and currently serves as Vice Chairman of the Investment Committee.

STEPHEN J. DARBY, JR.

Executive Vice President
United States Trust Company of New York

As head of the Asset Management Business Development Division for U.S. Trust, Mr. Darby directs the sales and marketing of all asset management services for institutions and individuals. Mr. Darby came to U.S. Trust in 1991 from Axe-Houghton Management, Inc., where he was President and CEO. He joined Axe in 1984, after more than ten years with Massachusetts Financial Services Co., where he was a Vice President and Assistant Director of the Investment Counsel Division in charge of marketing and client relations. Mr. Darby is a founding member of the Investment Marketing Forum and serves on the Advisory Board of the Plan Sponsor Network. He is a past President and former member of the Advisory Council and Advisory Board of AIMSE.

Mr. Darby holds a B.A., cum laude, from Hofstra College and attended New York University School of Law.

DAVID A. DAVENPORT

Assistant Treasurer
Lord Corporation

Mr. Davenport has been Assistant Treasurer with Lord Corporation since 1989 where he is responsible for bank relations, debt strategy, risk management, foreign exchange, and pension management. Previously, he was Manager, Domestic Treasury Operations with Baush & Lomb in Rochester, New York for ten years.

Mr. Davenport is the author of *The Equity Manager Search* (Quorum 1989). He has also published articles on manager searches in *Corporate Cashflow* and *Investing*.

Mr. Davenport received his B.S. degree in Economics from the University of Pittsburgh and an M.B.A. in Finance from Lehigh University.

ARJUN DIVECHA

Director, Information Technology Services
BARRA

Mr. Divecha is currently coordinating the development of BARRA's new Emerging Markets Model. He also organizes, coordinates, and speaks at seminars around the world. Mr. Divecha joined BARRA in 1981 as a Consultant and was initially involved with the development of the AURORA Equity Analysis System. He was subsequently Director of Equity Services and was responsible for marketing and client support for BARRA's U.S.-based equity clients.

Mr. Divecha received an M.B.A. in finance from Cornell University in 1981, with an emphasis on investments. He also attended the Indian Institute of Technology and graduated with a Bachelor of Technology in Aeronautical Engineering.

DAVID L. EAGER

Managing Partner
Eager & Associates

Mr. Eager co-founded Eager & Associates in 1984. The firm provides marketing research and management consulting to investment management firms. The firm has been a pioneer with both its Client Satisfaction Studies and its annual Benchmarks Study of investment industry operations and marketing. Formerly, Mr. Eager was National Director of Asset Planning Services for William M. Mercer, Inc. and was a Senior Consultant with A.G. Becker (now SEI Funds Evaluation). He began his career as an in-house money manager, responsible for trust investments and investor relations at Gerber Products Company.

NICK MENCHER

Institutional Marketing Manager
G.T. Capital Management, Inc.

Mr. Mencher is Institutional Marketing Manager for G.T. Capital Management, Inc. in San Francisco, California. Formerly a Senior Consultant with BARRA, he has also worked for Institutional Investor and was the waterfront reporter for the *Gloucester* (Mass.) *Daily Times.* Mr. Mencher's articles on finance and pension fund issues appear in numerous North American, European, and Asian publications, and he is currently Managing Editor of a new journal published by Institutional Investor.

A graduate of Colby College and Columbia University, he was associate editor, with Frank J. Fabozzi, of *Pension Fund Investment Management* (Probus 1990).

HUGH M. NEUBURGER

Private Consultant

Mr. Neuburger is a private consultant based in Greenwich, Conn. Earlier in his career, he was a founder and managing director of Matrix Capital Management and an Assistant Professor in the Columbia University Graduate School of Business. Mr. Neuburger is the author of numerous scholarly articles in the fields of macroeconomics, applied econometrics, and finance. He has worked for more than a decade on financial applications of time series statistics.

Mr. Neuburger holds a Ph.D. from the University of Chicago.

DOUGLAS B. REEVES

Senior Vice President
Dain Bosworth, Inc.

Mr. Reeves was Chairman of the investment committee for the Wyoming State Pension Board of Trustees. He has been active in the securities industry, currently serves on the Association of Securities Dealers, and is the former chairman of that region. Mr. Reeves was the founder of an investment advisory and securities firm, and is now Senior Vice President of Dain Bosworth, Inc.

He holds degrees from the University of Southern California and the University of Wyoming, and serves on the adjunct business faculty of the Regis University M.B.A. program.

CHRISTINE M. RØSTVOLD

President
Charnley & Røstvold, Inc.

In 1978, Ms. Røstvold co-founded Charnley & Røstvold, Inc., a consulting firm that assists investment management organizations with strategic planning, product positioning, and programs for tax-exempt plans. Charnley & Røstvold, Inc., has worked with more than 125 different investment management groups, encompassing a wide range of firms.

Prior to forming Charnley & Røstvold, Ms. Røstvold was with Collins Associates, a consulting firm specializing in investment manager search programs. She was responsible for research on alternative investment services such as real estate, option writing, index funds, money market funds, guaranteed insurance contracts, and international management. Ms. Røstvold coordinated investment management presentations at Collins Associates' offices and attended corporate committee manager research and quarterly client meetings.

She received her bachelor's degree in History from the University of California at Irvine.

L. DUNCAN SMITH

Senior Vice President
Frank Russell Company

Mr. Smith joined Frank Russell Company in 1983 as a Client Executive. His primary work is in the manager research process, and current responsibilities include U.S. equity, international equity, and fixed income. In addition, he is head of the Russell Private Investments department.

Mr. Smith was a consultant with Peat, Marwick, Mitchell & Co. from 1976 to 1983. He specialized in their investment supervision consulting practice and was administrative principal of that unit.

From 1964 to 1976, Mr. Smith was a Director, Executive Vice President in charge of all branch offices, and head of a national marketing staff for Lionel D. Edie & Co., an investment management firm. He worked for Texas Instruments, Inc.'s apparatus division from 1958 to 1964. From 1955 to 1958, Mr. Smith was with E.I. duPont as an engineer.

Mr. Smith holds a B.S. in mechanical engineering from Purdue University.

AMIE DIXON STAMBERG

President
Stamberg Prestia Ltd.

Ms. Stamberg co-founded Stamberg Prestia Ltd. in 1989 to focus on creating and marketing innovative financial products, including the Minority Equity Trust. The Trust is managed by nine minority- and women-owned investment advisors.

In 1987, she founded Stamberg & Associates Ltd. to provide a broad array of consulting services to institutional money management firms.

Formerly a partner at Fairfield Capital Associates, she was also a Vice President at the Frank Russell Company.

Ms. Stamberg attended Smith College and the University of Madrid. She holds a B.A. in Economics from the University of Texas, and an M.B.A. in Finance from the University of Washington.

CURTIS VOSTI

Reporter
Pensions & Investments

Mr. Vosti has been a *Pensions & Investments* reporter since 1988. Prior to that, he reported on business and labor in northwest Indiana for *The Hammond Times*, and freelanced in Washington D.C., while writing his master's thesis.

Mr. Vosti has an M.A. from the University of Missouri School of Journalism and a B.A. in American History from the University of Illinois.

SUSAN B. WEINER, PH.D.

Consultant on Japanese Business

Susan B. Weiner, Ph.D., is a West Newton, Mass. consultant to American companies doing business with Japan. She formerly managed external communications and Japanese business development for an investment management firm with U.S. equity mutual funds for Japanese clients. She has run a course on "How to Make Money in the Japanese Stock Market" for the Boston Security Analysts Society.

Dr. Weiner attended the University of Tokyo on a Fulbright Fellowship.

Marketing Investment Management Services in the 1990s

NICK MENCHER

Institutional Marketing Manager,
G.T. Capital Management, Inc.

Life in the investment management business is getting tougher. A variety of factors has led to the shrinking of institutional demand for managers, an increase in competition, and a growing obsolescence of traditional marketing methods. This book seeks to arm money managers with the tools they will need to win, and keep, institutional accounts in the 1990s.

Managers seeking to make inroads into traditional defined benefit pension funds are finding that a variety of forces have reduced the industry's explosive growth of the 1970s and 1980s. According to a study by Sanford C. Bernstein & Co., growth in the investment management field is likely to occur at between one-half and two-thirds of the rate the industry enjoyed during the period of 1974 to 1990. The result, according to the study, is that "More of the industry's growth will be captured by fewer managers in the next five years than in the past five."[1]

According to Michael Goldstein, author of the study, success in the money management field will rely on marketing, which he called the "key" to the field at this point, adding that successful management firms of the future would need to put more resources than ever into marketing.[2]

Manager marketing efforts—including sales materials, advertising, presentation skills, and the proposal process—will now play an increasingly important role as a growth industry matures and competition increases.

Overfunded Plans Mean Less Opportunity

The contraction of demand has many sources—perhaps the major one is overfunded plans. As many plans become fully funded, the industry seems headed for a period of increased competition for existing, rather than new, assets.

According to a survey of 383 Fortune 500 companies, eighty-nine percent had fully funded or overfunded plans relative to vested benefit obligations for fiscal 1990.[3] Their liability needs met, many funds are turning to long-duration, fixed income instruments seeking to protect their gains. While this is good news for fixed income managers, who have seen their business grow in recent years, it tends to leave equity managers, especially U.S. equity managers, out in the cold.

The decline in contributions to both public and private pension funds, the lifeblood of new business for managers, will further limit opportunities for those seeking pension fund clients.

Contributions to corporate funds have been sluggish for several years. For all companies surveyed, dollar amounts were as follows: 1986, $35.9 billion; 1987, $33.9 billion; 1988, $40.5 billion; 1989, $34.2 billion; and projected 1990, $38.0 billion. The drop among the largest corporations—traditionally the source of much business for many managers—is particularly evident. For the 200 largest companies in the Fortune 500, the figures are as follows: 1986, $19.2 billion; 1987, $18.1 billion; 1988, $15.7 billion; 1989, $15.9 billion; and projected 1990, $16.2 billion. In fact, as we will see later, smaller companies may offer the most opportunity in the 1990s.

Public fund contributions have also been relatively flat for several years. After jumping from $30 billion in 1986 to $32.4 billion in 1987 and $47.4 billion in 1988, 1989's figure was $49.0 billion, and 1990's is estimated to be $44.6 billion.[4]

New Managers Join the Ranks

Given these factors, it would seem that opening new management shops would be a dubious business venture. But every year, new shops open—all striving to compete for a piece of the same shrinking pie. While some types of managers are finding their business is increasing—particularly international stock and bond managers—the business is becoming more concentrated and both existing and new managers who do not distinguish themselves by innovative products or marketing approaches may not fare well in this environment.

The business is also seeing growing competition between asset classes. As sponsors increase their allocations to international stocks and bonds, consider specialized classes like managed futures and timberland, and lock in gains with fixed income portfolios, existing managers can find their accounts reduced when funds reallocate assets.

Managers are also facing competition from an unlikely source—corporations whose officers have managed assets in-house, and are now running money for outside clients. While this new line of business is not yet a major threat to established managers, several large corporations have spun off new companies that compete, to varying extents, with established managers.

Supply Outstrips Demand

Not only is competition increasing, demand is shrinking. Of the forty-two percent of funds which hired managers in 1990, the mean number hired was 2.2. Of the thirty percent of funds which fired managers in 1990, the mean number terminated was 1.7. In 1990, according to

Greenwich Associates, forty percent of corporate funds reported hiring managers, and thirty-eight percent said they would hire managers in 1991.

For public funds, forty-seven percent had hired, and forty percent planned to hire in 1991.

Overall, only forty-one percent of funds planned to hire managers, and over half of these funds said they would pick only one new manager in 1991.

Marketing efforts will become even more critical in this era of declining hiring plans by institutions. One of the key roles in the manager hiring process is played by the pension consultant.

The Consultant's Role

The pension consultant has long played a powerful role in the lives of managers. By advising pension funds on manager searches and hiring, the consultant-aided manager search process has functioned as a de facto marketing service for managers, and has resulted in managers marketing themselves directly to consultants. While managers must stress consultant relations as a key part of their marketing efforts, relying entirely on consultants for marketing has its limitations when in-house searches bypass the use of consultants.

According to Eager & Associates, in-house searches have increased in recent years. In 1988 they represented twenty-four percent of overall searches. In 1989 the figure had increased to twenty-nine percent, and by 1990 in-house searches were thirty-two percent of all searches.

Increasing in-house manager searches are part of an overall industry trend toward unbundling full-service consulting relationships, and, for some sponsors, taking consultant tasks in-house.[5] In-house searches represent a marketing challenge for managers. Unless the firm is well known or markets itself aggressively, it is difficult for managers who have relied principally on consultants to succeed with in-house searches. To help remedy this situation, managers may want to seek inclusion in the databases maintained for use by sponsors doing in-house searches.

Other methods include knocking on doors, cold-calling plan sponsors, speaking at seminars and conferences, advertising, public relations, and hiring house economists to work with clients and portfolio managers. Even video and data diskette presentations have been offered as a way of reaching out to plan sponsors. All these solutions, however, pose problems for smaller managers with meager marketing budgets, and it must be noted that some observers see a bleak future for smaller managers whose resources may not be up to the challenges posed by their deeper-pocketed colleagues.

In the international arena, consultants have played a dominant role. Because managers hail from diverse regions and handle assets many U.S. sponsors are unfamiliar with, most sponsors have brought in consultants to handle searches. Consultants, faced with slowing searches for active U.S. equity managers, are happy to fill the need and see increasing competition for accounts providing value-added for funds. One consultant advises managers seeking new business in the increasingly crowded international field to stand out from the crowd by stressing the unique features of their process and products.[6]

The Search for New Fields

Some managers are looking for new markets by targeting the estimated $1 trillion held by insurance companies. One advantage in exploring this area is the insurance industry's traditional long-term view of investment performance, and thus, it is hoped, long-term employment of managers by insurance companies. But the insurance market is not a free lunch. The differing tax and accounting regulations make transitions by ERlSA-focused money managers difficult.

The explosive growth of defined contribution plans in the 1980s has created a pool of nearly $500 billion. Most of these assets have traditionally been invested in highly risk-averse instruments. However, recent concerns over the safety of these securities means increasing potential for shifts to U.S. and international equities and an increase in demand for managers. A further boost to equity investment is forecast as educational efforts for plan members drive home the need to hold some assets in equities to create retirement assets that allow a reasonable post-retirement standard of living. Recent governmental regulations encouraging employers to offer several investment options to defined contribution plan members are also expected to spur equity investing.

Some observers see this market as a must for new managers. "It used to be new managers could focus exclusively on the defined benefit market." wrote Grant Kalson in a *Pensions & Investments* Commentary.[7] "This no longer is the case. Those doors increasingly are shut because of declining new cash flow and plan terminations. The defined contribution market also is tough to penetrate. But the potential cash flow in this market suggests strongly the effort might pay off."

Competition from large mutual fund firms for defined contribution assets is daunting, however, and smaller firms will need to work hard to market their ability to add value in the defined contribution arena.

Another pool of new business managers are looking towards is the prefunding of retiree health care costs—estimated to total anywhere from $400 billion to $3 trillion.[8] When FAS 106 goes into effect next year, corporations will need to reflect post-retirement health benefits on their balance sheets. While a variety of tax and legal issues need to be worked out, the prospect of special funds set aside to pay for these liabilities is receiving attention from managers.

According to some observers, equity managers stand to benefit most from FAS 106 and prefunding. This is because the soaring costs of medical liabilities may require sponsors to take on more risk to match the future cost of medical benefits.

Other managers are seeking the promised land north and south of the border. As Canadian legislation allows pension funds to invest larger portions of their assets in non-Canadian equities, international and U.S. managers are racing to establish a presence in the region to compete for new allocations. Others are looking with interest at developments in Latin America—where changes in some governmental pension structures may create a need for U.S.-based equity managers. Some managers, remembering the long, expensive, and painful fight to gain access to Japanese pension money, and the disappointing results, are tempering their optimism with caution.

Targeting New Funds for Marketing

Other areas managers might investigate are the smaller private and public funds. Many of these funds are beginning to branch out into asset classes which were formerly the domain of larger funds. For example, while only thirteen percent of corporate funds larger than $1 billion planned to start investing in international stocks in 1990, twenty-one percent of plans in the $100 to $250 million range planned to add international equities.

And when public funds were asked whether they would start using international stocks in 1990, the largest group to respond affirmatively were the smallest plans—those under $50 million in size. These results are partially a function of the fact that many of the larger funds are already invested in this area. For example, fifty-five percent of large public funds were invested in international stocks in 1990 as opposed to thirteen percent of smaller plans.

Nonetheless, managers who pass up the smaller universe may miss one of the last major growth areas for the industry. The demand by smaller funds for investments is not confined to international stocks—smaller corporate and public funds planned to start using U.S. growth and small-cap stocks at rates higher than their larger-cap brethren.[9]

International equity managers were heartened to hear that cracks were appearing in one of the last bastions of U.S.-only investing when the Massachusetts State Carpenters Pension Fund hired two international equity managers, and, according to trade press reports, did "what virtually all union funds will not allow themselves to do—invest actively in non-U.S. capital markets."[10] Union funds, traditionally shunned by international money managers, represent an untapped resource of some $190 billion. Many international managers are re-thinking their marketing strategy in light of this development.

Another marketing possibility for managers is to publicize their success in reducing transaction costs. Following a 1987 Department of Labor ruling on the need to reduce trading costs, this area has become increasingly important to sponsors. By using portfolio trading systems and other methods to reduce transaction costs, active managers may be able to gain some ground on their passive brethren who have benefited by their ability to hold transaction costs to a minimum.

One area not discussed in detail here, but which is starting to heat up, is the estimated $500 billion held by high-net-worth individuals. These wealthy people may be a strong market for managers. One concern is portfolio size—many portfolio managers prefer to manage separate accounts of more than $10 million or so, and this can deter many of even the highest net-worth individuals. To tap this market, and to gain exposure to the defined contribution field, some managers who have traditionally stayed away from mutual funds are beginning to offer management services through these investment vehicles.

The Manager as Advisor

Another new area for managers is as fund advisor—where managers advise funds on asset allocation, stock research, and trading techniques. The trades are then done by in-house fund managers.

While this form of management is growing slowly and is primarily popular among large corporate funds, it does represent a new market for managers. As more funds adopt in-house management, and increase sponsor sophistication, the manager-as-advisor relationship can be expected to grow.

Some evidence of this development is on hand. Public fund management of passive equities using managers and consultants in an advisory capacity rose from eight percent of funds in 1986 to forty percent of funds in 1988, (the most recent year for which data is available) whereas use of external managers stayed flat at around twenty-nine percent of funds. The growth in public fund use of advisory services for active common stocks and growth stocks has been flat for the last few years, but is still extensive.

Conclusion

The heady days of the 1970s and 1980s are over. Money managers who prosper in the leaner years to come will be the ones who pay attention to marketing in all its traditional manifestations—sales presentations, collateral materials, the proposal process, advertising, mailings and so on. While perfect foresight would be needed to divine the overall future of the industry—market performance, asset class popularity, and structural changes—one lesson is clear; managers who short the marketing process do so at their own peril.

NOTES

[1] "Money Management's Brave New World," *Institutional Investor,* March 1991, pp. 39–44.

[2] "Marketing, Visibility Vital Tools," *Pensions & Investments,* February 4, 1991, p. 17.

[3] Data Source: Hewitt Associates' report: *Pension Plan Disclosure Under FASB No. 87*. For these funds the median vested benefit obligation funded ratio was 133%; the median accumulated benefit obligation funded ratio was 125%; and the median projected benefit obligation funded ratio was 104%.

[4] Data Source: Greenwich Associates 1991 Report: *Investment Management: Going Global, Good Going*, pp. 18–20.

[5] "Why the thrill is gone from consulting," *Institutional Investor*, March, 1991, pp. 105–110.

[6] "Global Free-For-All," *Institutional Investor*, April, 1991, pp. 87–90.

[7] "Make Room for New Managers," *Pensions & Investments*, February 4, 1991, p. 14.

[8] "Absorbing the retiree health care hit," *Institutional Investor*, December 1991, pp. 101–104.

[9] Data Source: Greenwich Associates 1991 Report: *Investment Management: Going Global, Good Going*, p. 54.

[10] "Union Fund Goes Int'l! MA Carpenters Tap Two," *Investment Management Weekly*, December 9, 1991, p. 2.

2

Changing Players and Roles in the Institutional Money Management Industry

ARJUN DIVECHA

Director,
Information Technology Services,
BARRA

There has been rapid change in the institutional investment management industry during the last fifteen years. Is the period of rapid change over, or has it merely functioned as an introduction to a new pace of change? Some answers may emerge through an examination of the forces of competition that shape the industry.

This article presents a framework to understand some of these forces. We look at shifts of power between sponsors, managers, and brokers and conclude that sponsors are taking greater control of their funds at the expense of managers and brokers. This is manifested through increased shareholder activism, the use of performance fees, moving funds to passive and in-house portfolios, and taking greater control of soft dollars. We look at potential new entrants, particularly large, well-capitalized corporations, that might benefit from these changes.

We think it likely that brokers will be further squeezed by these changes and that consultants will play an important but different role as sponsors become more empowered. We look at the intensity of rivalry within the industry and conclude that the low levels of price competition for active management are not likely to persist and, as competition heats up, marketing will play a bigger role in the money management industry. Finally, we believe that regulatory bodies may well play a larger role in determining policy and funding levels in the industry.

We use the framework shown in Figure 1[1] to examine the competitive forces that shape the industry. At the center are the existing players—the established investment managers. The biggest impact on these players comes from their sponsors. We will look at the role sponsors play in determining profitability in the industry. Then there are potential entrants into the business and the barriers to entry that impede them. Other forces are ser-

FIGURE 1 / A Competitive Look at Investment Management

EXTERNAL INFLUENCES

New Players

Foreigners
Corporations

Suppliers

Brokers
Information
and Research
Services
Soft Dollars

Barriers to Entry,
Intensity of Rivalry

Buyers

Sponsors
Corporations
Individuals

Bargaining
Power of
Suppliers

Investment
Management

Institutional

Active | Passive

Retail

Bargaining
Power of
Buyers

Threat of
Substitute
Services

Substitutes

In-house
Management
Brokers
Consultants
Passive (?)

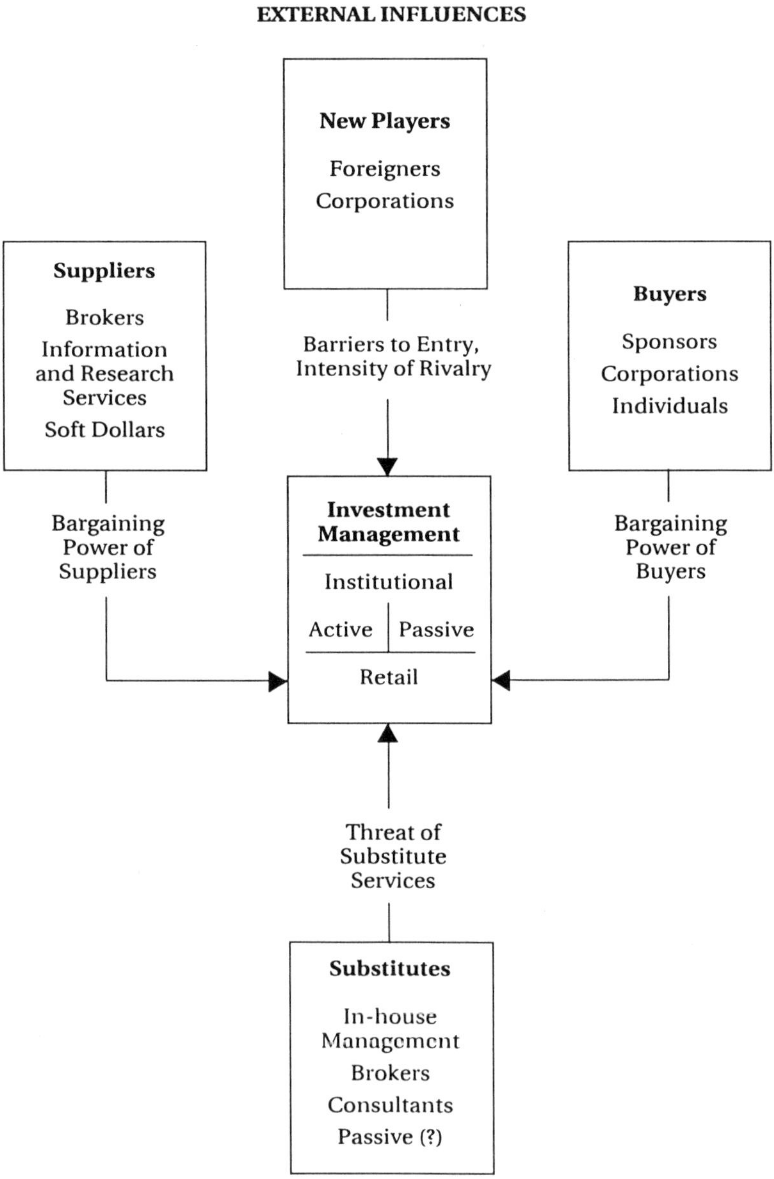

vices that represent substitutes to traditional investment managers. Finally, there are the brokers, consultants, and information providers whose business activities affect the day-to-day operations of investment managers.

The Bargaining Power of Sponsors

Who are the consumers in this industry? In the United States they are mainly private, state, endowment, foundation, and union pension funds. In Japan, corporate (or tokkin) funds play a big role. The empowerment of consumers over the last fifteen years extends into the sponsor community, with the field's primary consumers starting to flex their muscles and creating a source of pressure on the industry.

The power and influence of sponsors is tied to their size. For example, large sponsor organizations get a better deal from managers through declining fee schedules and, while performance evaluation is an inexact science, its development is allowing larger funds to begin using performance-based fees to control expenses. This process is abetted by the increasing sophistication of sponsors and their hands-on running of funds. This interest itself is a source of pressure; an educated consumer can mean trouble for a complacent industry.

One reason sponsors have become more sophisticated is the large growth of assets. This, along with changes in accounting standards (such as FASB 87), have forced corporations to look longer and harder at the role the pension fund plays in the corporation. Greater resources are being employed here, with the pension area offering a more credible career path for bright people. This has led to a greater realization among sponsors that control of the overall structure of the fund is a problem that cannot be delegated to their managers. It is not enough to pick good managers; one must also make sure that they add up to something coherent. This is evident from increased interest in asset allocation, risk control, and normal portfolios.

The bargaining power of sponsors is particularly high for passive management, but there is also a movement toward lower fees for active management. Fee pressure exists both from corporate and public pension plans. In one recent public fund search for an international active equity manager, the desire of the sponsor to pay lower than usual fees, along with complaints from some managers, received prominent coverage in the trade press. One may also argue that performance fees are simply a subtle way of reducing average fees in the industry.

We also see sponsors beginning to wrest control of soft dollars from their managers. The issue is clear: Should managers pay for research out of their own operating revenues, or from the client's money? If soft dollars disappeared, who would pay for research services, and would the price of these services then increase or decrease?

In summary, it appears that greater awareness among sponsors has led to greater control of the investment process. This has come at the expense of investment managers, and the trend appears likely to persist.

New Players

The business of investment management is unique. What other industry can claim such low start-up costs? It almost seems that one person, a telephone, a friendly broker, and a good marketing spiel do an investment manager make. Low start-up costs have fueled the large growth of small boutique firms in the past decade. Will this growth persist, or are we more likely to see large foreign and domestic corporations become major new entrants? We see some evidence of the latter.

For many years now, U.S. sponsors have hired foreign managers to manage international assets. Recently, Japanese and European managers have been gaining experience in the U.S. market by managing funds for their home markets.[2] Given the low levels of price competition for active management products, these foreign managers seem good prospects to enter the business. However, a more important question may be whether U.S. investment managers will be major players in the burgeoning foreign markets, especially Japanese and United Kingdom funds. The issue of whether U.S. firms will be able to offset increasing competition at home by increasing market penetration abroad is a worthwhile subject for review.

Another trend we see is pension funds being spun off by corporations as separate subsidiaries. This allows them not only to be more creative in structuring employee compensation packages but also to enter the business of managing money for other sponsors. These funds will now be able to either reduce expenses through economies of scale or become profit centers. Indeed, in recent years we have seen some of the largest pension funds in the world start to manage money for smaller pension funds.

Given the entrepreneurial nature of the business and low start-up costs, we still expect to see a large number of small boutiques opening their doors, although fewer than the last decade has spawned.

Another shift in the industry comes from the movement toward defined contribution plans and away from defined benefit plans. One impact of this has been to open the door for large mutual fund organizations to manage money that (under defined benefit plans) might have gone to institutional managers. Indeed, we see evidence that the large mutual fund organizations are becoming major players in the institutional business.

What barriers to entry do these potential new entrants face when trying to gain a foothold in the industry?

Barriers to Entry

Typical barriers to entry include economies of scale, product differentiation, capital requirements, switching costs, access to distribution channels, and the impact of external regulatory bodies.

Economies of scale are especially critical in passive management. There are definite scale economies in most operational aspects of passive management, such as portfolio construction and back-office operations. Even in trading, where there may be diseconomies of scale for active managers, passive management still reaps the benefits of size since most trading is price insensitive.[3] In addition, indexers with many accounts can cross trades internally, leading to greater efficiencies. As a result, passive management has become a commodity product, where the costs of production are the major determinant of price. However, sauce for the goose is sauce for the gander; we consequently see many sponsors starting to manage passive money in-house. With the increasing availability of easy-to-use portfolio management tools and package trading, the decision to switch to in-house management has become progressively easier in the last few years.

Up to a point, the same scale economies apply to active management. However, almost all active approaches have a finite depth and liquidity constraints beyond which value is hard to add. For any given strategy, diseconomies of scale may actually exist when a particular level of assets under management is reached.[4] Nevertheless, the marginal cost of taking on additional funds is still very small, so we see declining fee schedules serving as barriers to new managers.

One area where new entrants to most industries can successfully enter a market is in neglected or ignored niches. But given that there are more than two thousand investment managers in the United States alone, it seems unlikely that such niches exist. In addition, there are strong, established customer loyalties in the business which further hamper access by new managers.

New managers must also confront the need for an established reputation and a successful track record— perhaps the greatest barriers to entry. We can see why many of the new players are, in fact, old players in new suits—those portfolio managers who leave one firm to "satisfy their entrepreneurial urges," as the expression goes, by starting their own firms; often by taking some of their old accounts with them. This has led to a type of "apprenticeship" system in the business. For truly "new" managers, the need for a successful track record leads to a Catch-22 situation. This may benefit large corporations who can "buy" experience by buying managers, provided they can come up with creative compensation schemes to attract and keep top talent. Marketing can play a key role here by helping new managers establish credibility despite brief track records, and by convincing sponsors to invest in innovative, but untested, strategies.

In most businesses there are often high start-up costs and capital requirements. In traditional active equity management, there are high costs of having teams of analysts, portfolio managers, and large back-office staffs. For quantitative and process-driven money managers, however, the growth of computerized investment tools and back-office systems have enabled some firms to manage $4 billion with a staff of only twenty people. Clearly, capital in the form of money is not a major barrier to entry (or success). Rather, it appears that human capital is key.

Low capital requirements are likely to change if performance fees become the norm. One impact of performance fees will be to increase the business risk of money management,[5] leading to a situation where investment managers will have to be far more highly capitalized than they currently are. This again makes a case for large corporations with deep pockets to enter the business, driving out small, undercapitalized boutiques.

Another barrier to entry is the financial and emotional cost of switching from one manager to another. Industry practice is to give managers at least three to five years for their ideas to succeed or fail. There are also trading costs involved in switching managers. Perhaps the biggest switching cost comes from the difficulty in identifying good managers. During the 1980s, the cost of switching was not a major barrier to entry because the large net inflow of funds into the business meant sponsors could allocate funds to new managers without having to replace existing managers. This is not likely to persist if there is no growth in net assets, and the current levels of overfunding and an aging population make it unlikely that we will see much growth in funds from the pension market in the next decade.

Clearly, access to distribution channels is an important variable in garnering new business. Given the multitude of investment managers, the hardest part is often getting in the door. Consultants have effectively become gatekeepers, and being *qualified* by these firms is crucial. In addition, *true* performance evaluation is very difficult, making it hard to be certain that a particular manager is good or bad (as opposed to lucky or unlucky), thereby making it harder to displace established managers.

Finally, there is the role of regulatory bodies. Unlike other professions, where board certifications and advanced degrees serve as an absolute barrier to entry, there are few legal requirements to become a money manager. Being a CFA helps, but by no means is it considered essential.

In addition, the United States market is freely open to all comers because there has been minimal interference from the Securities Exchange Commission, Department of Labor, etc. But it is not clear that this will always be the case. In the post-crash environment, there were many calls for regulation. As the pension pie has grown and with scandals in the public eye, there will be a greater tendency for politicians to get involved. We expect increasing interference from politicians and special-interest groups in coming years. This will work for firms in the industry that have the resources to deal with these non-investment and regulatory issues.

Overall, compared to other industries, the barriers to entry are low. The thickness of manager directories is a testament to this. The few barriers that do exist have more to do with reputation and credibility than economies of scale and capital requirements.

The Threat of Substitute Products and Services

What role do substitute products and services play in threatening established players? In our opinion, the largest threat to investment managers is sponsors taking money in-house. One of the goals of marketing in the 1990s will be to convince sponsors that in-house management is not always the best path to follow.

One can separate money management into three functional areas: research, portfolio construction, and trading. All three traditionally have been the domain of managers, but to improve performance and to control costs, one can see sponsors taking on some or all of these functions. Sponsors may buy ideas, manage portfolio construction and trading themselves, or delegate one or more of these individual aspects to specialist managers.

The benefits of in-house management have been well documented, with low costs being one of the largest. Other factors encouraging the trend are the increased professionalism of sponsors and creative compensation structures for in-house managers. We see the trend of sponsors managing passive funds internally spreading to active or process-driven (as opposed to judgement-driven) portfolio management.

Brokers and consultants now play a role in managing funds by selling package trading and portfolio management tools such as dedication, immunization, and indexing directly to sponsors. We also see a trend of sponsors directly buying strategies from "idea shops" and implementing these in-house. Will packaged passive management originated by brokers be next?

Consultants have had an influential role in the industry by recommending management approaches, managers, and asset allocation strategies that may include new asset classes outside the traditional areas of many managers. As fund management moves further away from purely domestic stock/bond/cash combinations, managers specializing in these fields will continue to feel the heat from specialty managers in such fields as emerging markets, international bonds, etc. All these represent a threat to the narrowly focused manager who does not adapt to an expanding marketplace for ideas by improving both investment methods and marketing.

The Bargaining Power of Suppliers

Suppliers to the investment management industry are brokers, consultants, data and research vendors, information providers, and soft-dollar vendors.

Deregulation of fixed-rate commissions has had a long-term impact on the brokerage community. Explicit trading costs (per share) for equities have dropped dramatically in the last fifteen years. Even though volumes have increased since deregulation, the equity business is far less profitable today for brokers than it once was. Consequently, there appears to be a growing realization that research and execution are each going to have to pay their own way. This may lead some brokers to get out of providing research altogether, encouraging the growth of independent research consultants who pick up where the brokers leave off. Brokers are also being squeezed by the advent of computerized trading networks which threaten to impact the easier and more lucrative parts of their business. In fixed income trading, the large brokerage houses still have monopolistic control of the marketplace. Will this persist or will it go the way of equities? In this environment, only the brokers that can clearly demonstrate value-added to their clients are likely to remain as major suppliers to the institutional business.

Consultants have had a fairly large impact in the past few years. As sponsors become more sophisticated, the kind of consulting services they require will change. We see manager searches and asset allocation increasingly being done by in-house staffs and, as sponsors take greater control of the management process, consultants will be needed primarily for their expertise in using information, data, and quantitative tools. This reduces the power of consultants to act as gatekeepers and may have significant ramifications for traditional search consultants. The shift to in-house searches also calls for more marketing efforts on the part of managers.

With the proliferation of soft dollars has come a large number of small, independent firms providing computerized trading software, back-office systems, information and research services, and access to global securities data. Because of the large number of players, these services have increasingly become commodity products, and the real cost to investment managers has declined dramatically. One effect of this has been to reduce the costs of investment management substantially in the last decade. If soft dollars disappear and the industry becomes more competitive, we are likely to see a fair number of consolidations in this area.

Intensity of Rivalry

We have looked at the different external forces that shape the industry. But what can new entrants expect to find when they enter the field? How intense is the competition between managers, and how is the competitive environment changing? Some answers may emerge from a look at how large the field is, how rapidly the industry has grown, and other issues that affect profitability.

As mentioned earlier, there are large numbers of players in active management, while passive management is highly dominated by a few very large players. This is a natural consequence of the economies of scale in the passive business. Given that there may be diseconomies of scale in active management, it is possible that we will see consolidation in the industry from larger firms buying smaller specialized boutiques (as opposed to generalists).

In most industries, taking on incremental business generally requires an increase in capital or production facilities. Investment managers, however, can add new business with a very small increase in costs. Since the marginal cost of providing services is small, one would expect to find a high degree of price competition, but this is not the case for active management products. Why is this? It may have something to do with the rapid growth of the industry in recent years when it was possible to garner new accounts without getting into bidding wars with other managers.

Another possible reason for the lack of price competition is the difficulty in evaluating performance. For example, if one is buying a computer, you know with certainty what you will get in terms of performance. It is therefore easy to compare prices offered by different vendors. However, the uncertainties inherent in the investment business make it nearly impossible for sponsors to comparison shop for managers. Performance fees help remedy this situation by setting the fee ex-post rather than ex-ante, and marketing again plays a crucial role.

The record of the last fifteen years of pension fund contributions and asset growth has meant both minimal price competition and a compensation structure best described as "fat and happy" for the upper end of the business. The level of compensation in this industry can only be compared with investment banking.

But are today's managers actually sitting ducks? Is the current state of the investment management industry a parallel to Detroit in 1964? We think the industry may be vulnerable because growth has led to minimal price competition—a situation where an overseas push may occur. Recall the strategy that Japanese automakers used to penetrate the U.S. market started at the low end of the market and then moved up. The logical starting point in the investment management business would be passive and quantitatively driven products. The ability of firms to reduce costs and sustain low margins for long periods of time will be the key determinants of successful market penetration. Fortunately for existing money managers, the passive arena is the most efficient part of the market, making it much harder for new players to gain a foothold. If active managers believe their end of the business is not susceptible to attack, one only has to look at the auto industry: Japanese automakers are today successfully threatening high-end European imports.

Another factor determining competition are the strategic reasons to stay in a business even if it is unprofitable. Years ago, when a single bank provided all needed financial services to a corporation, one could have made the case for providing portfolio management as a service (even if it were unprofitable). Today, that situation does not exist, so there seems to be no compelling non-financial reason to stay in the investment management business. As a result, we have recently seen cases of large money-center banks selling their investment management businesses.

One inducement to enter the industry is the lack of penalties for leaving it. Exit barriers are minimal: there are few long-term labor contracts, no community impacts, no government or social pressures, and no capital-intensive structures to dismantle. As easy as it is to rent an office, fill it with plants, furniture, and computers, it is just as easy to lock the doors and walk away.

One conclusion we draw is that passive management is currently very competitive and efficient and, therefore, we are unlikely to see major changes in that part of the industry, other than that of sponsors taking money in-house. Active management appears to be headed for a bout of price competition that will almost certainly drive down margins. Marketing and client service will be key for firms that must show their value-added makes up for higher fees. While performance must contribute to value-added to offset higher fees, it is the job of the marketing/client service to communicate performance to prospects and clients.

Future Considerations

What do the next fifteen years have in store for the investment management industry? Here is a look at where new opportunities may lie and which forces are likely to have the greatest impact.

In other markets, corporate funds are a large part of the market. Will we see a similar movement in the United States market? As sponsors get more into the business of managing money, will the pension area become a profit center within the treasury function of a firm? Indeed, will we see a new breed of *merchant investors* as sponsors increase their involvement in the management of assets they own? In recent years we have seen large pension funds battle corporations in which they are significant shareholders for greater management control. There is little doubt that this trend will continue.

Given current levels of overfunding and demographics, it is unlikely that the United States pension market will grow as dramatically during the 1990s as it did in the 1980s. The greatest opportunities will probably lie in penetrating foreign markets, especially Japanese and United Kingdom pension and corporate funds. We see evidence of managers gearing up to market their services in these foreign markets. There is a strong perception that barriers to entry in these foreign markets are far greater than in the United States. Will these barriers be affected by the ongoing push by the United States to open up foreign markets?

Other new sources of funds, such as nuclear decommissioning trusts and the funding of health benefits, are likely to have a major impact on the growth of the business.

Trading is becoming crucial to both the buy and sell sides of the industry. We anticipate more services being offered to managers and sponsors to monitor trading effectiveness and reduce costs.

These are all areas from where we believe change will come. But perhaps the greatest pressure will come from increased competitiveness in a maturing industry.

Conclusion

The recent history of the investment management industry shows a wide range of fundamental changes. Looking ahead, we can expect additional changes caused by new entrants into the business and a greater competitiveness in the marketplace.

An examination of the forces operating in the investment management industry leads to the following conclusions:

- Barriers to entry into the field are low. They are not economic in nature, but have more to do with developing credibility and reputation;

- Little price competition exists outside of passive management, but forces among the sponsor community may change this—particularly in the form of performance fees and trading costs;

- Sponsors are taking greater control of their funds at the expense of managers, brokers, and consultants, and this will lead to further changes in the kinds of services they demand;

- The trend of sponsors managing passive funds internally will spread to active and process-driven (as opposed to judgement-driven) portfolio management;

- Performance fees will increase the capital requirements of the money management industry, perhaps leading to consolidations that result in fewer, more highly capitalized firms;

- Current scandals will result in a greater tendency for politicians and special-interest groups to get involved in investment management;

- There will be slower growth in the pension business, but new sources of funds, such as the funding of health benefits, may rival the pension market;

- Large corporations (both foreign and domestic) are likely to become larger players in the investment management business; and

- Low barriers to entry combined with easily transportable skills will cause continued high turnover in personnel, ensuring efficient circulation of fresh ideas and innovation.

NOTES

[1] Adapted from Michael E. Porter's book, *Competitive Strategy: Techniques for Analyzing Industries and Competitors,* The Free Press, New York, 1980, pp. 4–29.

[2] There are over 100 Japanese financial institutions that have set up offices in the United States to manage the U.S. component of their portfolios.

[3] Passive managers typically buy all or most components of the index irrespective of how hard it is to trade them.

[4] For example, small capitalization strategies have a much lower absorptive capacity than strategies that concentrate on larger stocks.

[5] For a further discussion of this topic, see Andrew Rudd's "Business Risk and Investment Risk," *Investment Management Review,* November/December 1987, pp. 19–27.

Marketing Strategies
•
Laying the Groundwork

The
Globalization
of a Cottage
Industry

KEN DOWD

ED MADDEN

Directors,
The Chemical Investment Group

The much-discussed "globalization" of the world's financial markets has had a rapid, highly visible impact in many sectors. In most, however, including institutional asset management, the most significant changes are only beginning to take hold. Considerable benefits and opportunities seem to be in store for investment managers worldwide.

Motivation

Perhaps the single most important change wrought by globalization has been the realization, for the first time, of an international institutional asset management "market"—and a staggering one it is, at an estimated value of $10 trillion. That's a lot of zeros, more than enough to motivate professional investment managers to find ways to capture some of them.

That the international pool of institutional funds is still mostly self-managed has not daunted professional managers because, concurrent with globalization, an increasingly complex web of exchange controls and other national constraints have dissolved. A trend toward deregulation in major financial capitals has heightened the pace of activity and competition. And a growing sophistication in many formative markets has resulted in greater emphasis on better return and improved risk, and a willingness to try new methods to achieve them. The role of the professional manager is being appreciated even in countries where few managers have ever practiced.

Technology

Of course, technology has the dazzle that gets much attention. Without instantaneous global communications, we could not have trading going on around the clock. Without high-speed computers and remarkable software, we could not operate on simultaneous local and multi-currency systems that investment managers are daily finding more essential.

Technology also drives some investment processes in a quantitative sense. Computers now screen and select stocks, and execute buy and sell orders, in any combination of dollars, yen, marks, or pounds sterling. Investment houses can now maintain data bases and screening models following currencies, interest rates, commodities, bonds, and more than ten thousand stocks with a minimum of fundamental staff research. And the results, for the most part, have been successful.

But what about the qualitative aspect of the investment process? Here, the changes brought about by globalization are as important as the technological ones, yet they are only beginning to be addressed.

Cross-Border Marketing

Marketing and sales functions in asset management are facing challenges that never existed before. Cross-border marketing was unheard of. The traditional professional manager attitude, in many cases, was to let the audience seek them out.

Large numbers of small "boutiques" have flourished in the U.S. market, specializing in limited products in order to operate with a high degree of focus and service. Literally thousands of these boutiques have certainly increased the noise level of competition. The din has become so great, in fact, that one might begin to question whether the resulting confusion is providing a service or a disservice for the large institutional buyers, which are denominated in hundreds. How are purchasers of institutional asset management services to make reasonable judgements?

Service is, after all, the real value-added of any professional capability. And service in a globalized institutional market means not only quality of operations and variety of products, but also a responsiveness to the specific needs of each client. What the buyers' needs are, and for what reason, should be more important than just what's "hot" or available in the smorgasbord of international finance.

The GIC Case

This is demonstrated by how certain products seem to cycle or appear in different markets at later times—a reflection of the level of maturity in each market. Experienced American asset managers, for example, will recall the early popularity of the "guaranteed investment contract" (GIC). Because the investments were backed by insurance company capital, principal values were protected from erosion—an ideal situation for pensions and profit-sharing plans—while fixed interest returns were higher than competing fixed income investments of comparable perceived risk.

While many American funds have moved on to more sophisticated vehicles, the GIC concept has lived on, and would now be thought of as a response to investor needs in areas such as the Pacific Basin. The appeal is always greatest among first-time buyers: the assets return higher yields than anything else locally available, yet the principal is safe.

This echo effect isn't simply an imitation of the American model, which is certainly the standard, but a realistic response to the conditions of each market. First-time professional buyers were in the United States years ago. The markets seem to evolve in very similar ways, but in different time frames.

Of course, this pattern offers considerable advantage to American investment managers who have "been there" and now want to bring their experience to new markets. The challenge that tempers that advantage, however, is the necessity of being flexible to the unique needs of the times, the regions, and the investors.

The Paradox of Size

It is interesting to note that many large, established investment firms, both American and European, have not been able to make significant inroads into the global institutional asset management market, despite strong international reputations. Part of the reason may be that old, entrenched "fiefdoms" within these companies lack the flexibility to respond to changing conditions, or the coordination to market services effectively on a global scale.

Size may offer considerable advantages in terms of leverage or a multitude of offices, but size is not always synonymous with coordinated sales and client service; nor does it alone offer a clarity of focus that encourages confidence among investors.

Despite the staggering $10 trillion size of the worldwide institutional asset market, it is still served by what may be described as the largest "cottage industry" in the world. No single firm can currently claim more than a fraction of a percent of the overall market as its own. Indeed, a one percent share of the market would mean an utterly gigantic operation—perhaps one too large to make decisions and to maintain the confidence of buyers.

Yet even if a company should achieve that one percent share, it still would not have achieved a presence to move the market through its own activities. Thus, this "cottage industry" is likely to remain richly diverse, with plenty of room for many strategies to work successfully.

The burden must fall on professional investment managers to devise a new, "elementary" process that better responds to the needs of first-time buyers in new markets.

Service and Performance

The benefit to investors is that they now have more reasoned choices available. Discerning investors with a bit of experience under their belts are certain to think these new opportunities a plus. New buyers, however, may find the situation somewhat migraine inducing. Who needs even more choices when they are only beginning to learn how to articulate their needs? How are they to quantify their benchmarks and risk tolerance? What is a fair way to prequalify?

In a market where there is a premium on being able to define just what you're looking for, the burden must fall on professional investment managers to devise a new, "elementary" process that better responds to the needs of first-time buyers in new markets, and educates them on their expanding opportunities. That basis for a solid, long-term partnership will not be established by performance alone. A commitment to service will be the key to getting and keeping clients. And as competition raises standards of excellence worldwide, investors should expect to demand it.

Developing a Media Strategy

EDWARD W. GASKIN

Media strategy is the process of designing an advertising plan of attack. This process—although subtle when compared to product, price, and creative decisions—is no less important. Companies have been able to improve sales simply by altering their media strategy. Poor strategy delivers poor results, and the time and expense of producing an advertising campaign is wasted. Correct planning delivers a competitive advantage not easily duplicated by competitors.

Most financial service companies under-advertise. The irony is that, in attempting to keep advertising expenses down, companies risk wasting most of their money by not achieving a "threshold of retention." Hence, the message is forgotten. Since most financial service companies use magazines and newspapers, this article will focus on media strategy as it relates to print media.

The Target Market

The first step in setting media objectives entails defining the target market, then defining your message. These are the questions you need to ask yourself:

- *Whom do you want to reach?* How are you defining your target market—by title, size of organization, or some other criteria? Not all companies refer to the same job by the same title, so your target person should be defined by job function or responsibility. The type of organization—taxable, tax-exempt, etc.— is also important. Size is also helpful in further focusing your target, i.e., market assets of $100 million or more.

- *Where is your target market located?* If regional, is it New York, the Midwest, or truly nationwide? If international, is it Japan, United Kingdom, or pan-European? If the publication has some circulation abroad, will it translate your ad into the appropriate language?

• *When is the best time to reach your prospects?* Is there a period when the buying process starts or stops? Often, products that require committee decisions slow down during the summer months. Is your product sold year-round, year-end, or quarterly?

• *What do you wish to say to your prospects?* A complex message may need to be communicated in print so that the prospect has time to read and study it. Is it a message with a broad audience (e.g., all companies with 401(k) plans) or a very selective audience (e.g., companies with $500 million or more in pension assets)?

Establishing Measurable Objectives

After answering these questions, you must set measurable objectives for the media plan. Many media plans fail because they do not have a clear objective by which to measure success or failure. Do you wish to create awareness of a new product? Then be specific, stating "Our objective is to create awareness of our product with seventy-five percent of our target market." This means that three out of four of the prospects in your target market should be able to identify your name with the product and list one benefit. Or you may state, "We want this advertising campaign to produce fifty qualified leads for our salespeople in the next quarter."

There are two major factors that will determine your plan's success: reach and frequency.

Reach

Reach is the average number of times a prospect is exposed to a message. If your objective is to create seventy-five percent awareness of your product among your target market, then your strategy must reach at least seventy-five percent of the target market. This assumes that every reader who receives the publication will see your ad— which is not a very good assumption. You will probably have to reach eighty to ninety percent of your target audience to achieve a seventy-five percent level of awareness. And that would require using full-page ads.

When examining a publication's circulation, you should check the following:

• How much of your target audience is included? How much is waste circulation, from your point of view?; and

• How much of the circulation is to paid subscribers?

There are two views on this last question. One says: if subscribers pay for the publication, they will read it. The other view says: if the publication is good, people will read it whether paid or unpaid.

Also ask: how much of the circulation is pass-along circulation? This is when one person reads a publication and passes it on to another. This is common for business magazines and newspapers in reception areas, or publications that are routed through offices.

You should be able to determine the reach of a publication by dividing the total circulation by the percentage of readers in your target market.

Another important concept in helping to develop reach calculations is duplication. If one magazine alone will not meet your reach goals, then you will have to add additional ones. Once you add a second vehicle to reach your target market, you will have some duplication. That is, the second publication will not reach one-hundred percent different prospects.

This brings us to cost per thousand (CPM). CPM is the cost to reach one thousand of your prospects. It must be remembered that CPM measures cost, not efficiency. The best advertising vehicle is not the cheapest, it is the one that will best accomplish your objectives. You must always ask yourself: cost per thousand of what, and is there some waste circulation? CPM is a tool to help evaluate alternative media strategies that accomplish your media objectives. It means nothing in isolation.

Frequency

Frequency is the average number of times a prospect will see your message. Reach and frequency are related. The larger the reach, the lower the frequency, and vice versa. This is due to budget limitations. Frequency is important because the retention of advertising is so low. Most readers will have forgotten having seen your ad within the same day. Learning and retention require repetition. It is one thing to remember seeing an ad; it is another to remember the message.

An important question relating to frequency is, "how consistently do your prospects read the publication?" This goes from very consistently (three out of four issues) to occasionally (one out of four). Regular readership makes it easier to accomplish frequency with one publication. Another problem some advertisers have is getting high frequency in a short period of time. Instead of waiting four weeks or four months for one magazine to run, you may use four magazines with high levels of duplication.

Common Frequency Mistakes

A mistake that many advertisers make is running one ad each month, and rotating monthly the product to be advertised. In this case, the product ad for cash management may be run in January, June, and December, with other product ads in between. No wonder the ad does not receive a good response: it was only run three times all year with six months in between.

Another common mistake is when firms are launching a product and decide to "run an ad." One ad will simply not produce the level of awareness or retention necessary to make the message stick. This is not to say that the ad will not get a response; it is to say that the company is not maximizing the competitive advantage of launching a new product. If one company launches a product with a one-time ad, and a competing firm launches a similar product a month later with a high-impact media campaign, prospects are more likely to associate the product development with the second firm and not the first.

Few advertisers can afford constant frequency in many publications. Therefore, many media planners use a concept called *flighting*. Flighting occurs when there is a concentration of advertising in bursts, with a hiatus in between.

All other things being equal, some advertising messages require greater frequency than others. Specifically:

* *New products* require greater frequency than established ones;

- *Image advertising* requires greater frequency than product advertising;

- *Complex messages* require greater frequency than simple ones;

- *Ads in publications with higher advertising to editorial ratios* require greater frequency than those with lower ratios;

- *Ads in news-oriented publications* require greater frequency than ads in more reflective publications; and

- *Ads in publications with shorter "shelf life"* require greater frequency than those with longer shelf life.

Being Seen

An important aspect of your media strategy is *getting your ad seen.* Beyond captivating your audience with the creativity of your message, its size, position, and the colors used will greatly determine its impact.

When you are doing your evaluation, you might assume that every one of your prospects that receives the publication has been reached. For this to be correct, you must be assured that each prospect *saw* your ad. A determining factor here is the size of your ad. Research has demonstrated that the larger the ad size, the larger the readership. If a two page color spread equals one-hundred percent readership, then a one-page ad equals eighty-six percent, and a one-half-page ad equals seventy percent. By reducing the ad size, you create two additional problems.

First, in order to accomplish your objectives, you will need to run more ads to make up the difference (say, the other thirty percent for a half-page ad). This is *more expensive* than running larger ads, because the larger the space, the smaller the relative cost. More importantly, larger ads have a disproportionately greater impact.

The second problem is image related. A company attempting to sell premium financial services or to convince prospects that it is a market leader may undermine its message by using small black-and-white ads.

Color is similar to ad size. In general, each additional color improves recall on the part of your prospects.

Positioning refers to where the ad is placed in the publication. Cover positions have slightly higher impact, as do right-hand pages. There is a trend toward creating odd positions, which may have higher impact, but the number of publications accepting them is still very limited.

Editorial

The editorial of a publication should play a role in developing your media strategy. There are both objective and subjective criteria here. As an advertiser, you are interested in who really reads a publication. There is a difference between a magazine designed for CFOs with a section on pensions and a magazine designed for pension fund administrators. Both magazines may have a high percentage of the right corporations reading them—but one is "the CFO's magazine," and the other is the "pension fund administrator's magazine."

Here are some things to consider when examining editorial:

- *What is the nature of the publication?* An *active* publication is one that is very news and time oriented. If it is not read quickly after it comes out, it is out of date. Active publications are good for launching new products, and mentioning new people, plants, and promotions. *Passive* media is more reflective; the publication has more permanence or shelf life. The publication can be read a few weeks or a few months later and still be relevant. Passive publications are good for ads that contain complex messages, high-tech products, or products which require very reasoned arguments.

- *Are readers responding?* Is the publication being talked about? Do readers respond to reader service cards? Does the publication receive letters to the editor or requests for reprints?

- *What is the format of the publication?* What does the editorial calendar look like? Does the publication have departments or columns that run regularly enough for you to plan advertising around them? What mood does the publication put the reader in?

- *How do readers describe the editorial?* Different adjectives may be significant, such as "practical," "credible," "educational," or "entertaining."

- *How carefully are the articles read?* How much time a reader spends with a publication is another good determinant of readership. Expect to find lower "time spent" numbers for active publications and higher numbers for passive publications.

- *How loyal are the readers?* Do they read every issue or only when there is an article of interest?

- *How influential are the readers?* The decision-making power of readers is also important. What percentage of the readers of the publication decided or had influence on the decision to buy your company's product? A publication may describe the decision-making powers of its readers in areas vital to you.

Creative Considerations

Creative considerations may play a role in determining which medium you use. If you need to get a message out within the next few days, you would eliminate most magazines. If your ad requires a high quality of color or fine screen reproduction, you would eliminate most newspapers. If your targets are regional, you may want to do "split runs"—using different ads in different regions of the country.

Media Considerations

One medium may be better for communicating your message than another—e.g., broadcast media is not effective for complex messages. Some media are more selective and therefore more cost efficient than others. Space, time, discount structure, closing dates, mechanical, and translations help vary across different media. And, of course, your budget may eliminate certain media choices.

Marketing Considerations

Finally, marketing considerations are critical:

- *The price of your product* may dictate promotion in prestige or status media. Conversely, the profit margins on certain products may determine how and where they are advertised. For example, a company marketing index funds would have a difficult time covering the cost of running large ads in the *Wall Street Journal*. Another price consideration is the ability of a firm to split promotional costs with regional offices or other departments.

- *Promotion comes into play* when, for example, your firm decides to run a sales contest for a particular product. The time frame of the contest may require heavy frequency in a relatively short time period— eliminating quarterly publications. You may also want to coordinate your advertising with your public relations effort when launching a new product.

- *Where the product is being distributed* and the nature of those sales may play a role in determining your media strategy. Perhaps you wish to pump up sales in a particular region and you need to support the sales staff with advertising.

- *Where the product stands in its life cycle* has an impact on your media decisions. A new product requires longer ads, explaining the features and benefits. This usually requires print media of a reflective nature. In later phases, your ads may become shorter and simpler in order to state the benefits relative to a competing product. In more mature phases, frequency may become the most important aspect as you try to keep your name and product in the forefront of all prospects.

Taking into account these factors will help you develop an effective media strategy. The ultimate goal is to get your message to the right people at the right time.

The author wishes to give special thanks to Harold Bennett of William R. Biggs/ Gilmore Associates.

Marketing Investment Management to Japan

SUSAN B. WEINER, Ph.D.
Consultant on Japanese Business

Copyright © 1991 by Susan B. Weiner, Ph. D.

The Japanese have lots of money. And American money managers want to get their hands on it. The stagnation of the U.S. pension market, the traditional cash cow for investment managers, makes Japan look mighty attractive.

Some American firms are winning Japanese institutional investors as clients. Japan is the largest single foreign source of assets—more than $24 billion—for U.S. money managers, according to a survey of U.S. investment managers published by *Pensions & Investments* in 1990. There's more Japanese money to be won. Most of it will go to Americans who understand that Japanese clients have special needs.

The Japanese Environment for Money Managers

You might expect pension funds to be your best bet as potential clients. But until recently Japanese pension funds have been off-limits even to *Japanese* investment management firms. Only Japanese life insurance companies and trust banks could manage pension funds.

Therefore, American money managers have turned to *tokkin* and investment trusts *(toshi shintaku)* managed or distributed by Japanese firms. *Tokkin* are funds in which corporations invest excess cash. Investment trusts are the Japanese equivalent of American mutual funds.

The passage of Japan's Investment Advisory Act in 1986 helped Americans by legitimizing the investment management industry. Until then Japanese investment management firms—as distinct from institutions such as insurance companies, trust banks, and securities companies—were largely unregulated and had an unsavory reputation. In 1983–1984 a nasty scandal, in which clients lost about ¥18 billion, erupted around the *Toshi Journal,* an investment advisory publication. This spurred the Ministry of Finance (MOF) to draft the Investment Advisory Act and to begin regulating the industry.

The act provides for registration of investment advisors (those who suggest a course of investment action) and for licensing of discretionary advisors (those who can implement their own investment policy). The act targeted Japanese firms, but by laying out guidelines for registration and licensing, the MOF opened the way for foreign investment management firms to enter the Japanese market by showing them a set of procedures to establish themselves in investment management.

Many American firms applied for registration as investment advisors and then for the more demanding qualification of discretionary advisor. These included investment management firms like Alliance Capital Management, Batterymarch Financial, and Fidelity; brokerage firms like Merrill Lynch and Shearson Lehman; insurance companies like CIGNA; and even a pension consulting firm, the Frank Russell Company. By the spring of 1987, according to the *Nikkei kin'yu nenpo '87 shunkigo,* about fifteen firms of American origin had registered as investment advisors.

The restrictions binding pension management have loosened more slowly. The Ministry of Finance and the Ministry of Health and Welfare (MHW) began a debate by mid-1988. MHW argued for breaking the monopoly of life insurance companies and trust banks over pension funds. MOF resisted. In 1989, the ministries agreed on liberalizing pension regulations, allowing corporations with pension funds meeting certain size and age limits to use investment management firms or even to manage assets in-house.

More recently, the government has allowed foreign companies to enter the Japanese investment trust market directly. S.G. Warburg & Co. Japan Ltd., Jardine Fleming Investment Advisors Japan Ltd., and MIM Tokyo K.K. were the first approved by MOF, with Fidelity Investments Japan Ltd. and Credit Suisse expected to follow soon. However, foreign firms lack the network needed to sell to the investment trusts' potential clients, who are mainly individuals, and so are likely to rely on Japanese distributors.

Which Americans Win Japanese Clients?

American investment managers appeal to Japanese clients because of the Americans' investment performance, experience in non-Japanese markets, and investment technology.

Japanese life insurance companies and trust banks have tended to produce uniform, modest (around eight percent) returns because of lack of competition and their conservative nature. But Japan's rapidly graying population is increasingly pressuring the government to exact high returns to fund the rapidly growing burden of pensions. The returns offered by some American firms tempt the Japanese. But, be aware that Japanese are used to steady returns. Despite your disclaimers, they firmly believe that past performance is a guarantee of future performance. As in the United States, it is illegal to guarantee a specific rate of return, but Japanese clients are often very disturbed by volatile returns.

Your Japanese clients won't be happy when you teach them about volatility, but they will look to you for education. Japanese investment managers have little experience outside their domestic market. They are gingerly investing in U.S. government bonds and blue-chip stocks. They have a lot to learn about other investments through information and training provided by foreigners.

Most Japanese clients will ask for a steady flow of information on American markets. They usually don't stop at reams of paper. They also want to send "trainees" to work at your firm for periods of perhaps six months to two years. You may worry that the Japanese will learn your business, then compete with you. This can't happen if you keep your firm on the leading edge of technology.

Japanese investment managers believe that technology might overcome their weaknesses. The Japanese investment management business sprang up almost overnight and suffers from a lack of experienced portfolio managers. If they can automate investment, they won't need so many portfolio managers. The Japanese are also anxious to learn about sophisticated investment techniques, such as hedging using futures and options, which don't have much of a history in Japan.

Japanese clientele for American fund management can be found among the leading Japanese financial institutions: securities firms, trust banks, and life insurance companies. Their relationships may take the form of fund management (such as funds which Putnam Management manages for Kankaku Securities), joint ventures (such as the June 1989 joint venture created between Wells Fargo Investment Advisors and Nikko Securities), or partial ownership of a U.S. investment manager (such as the Long Term Credit Bank of Japan's stake in Miller, Anderson & Sherrerd).

How do American investment managers find their Japanese clientele? Unlike America, Japan has no formal manager search procedure involving lengthy questionnaires about investment philosophy and performance. Traditionally, the process relied on relationships. A company would give its relevant business to the trust bank or securities firm in its interrelated business grouping *(keiretsu)*.

A few *keiretsu* firms have invested in U.S. brokerage firms, as with Sumitomo and Goldman Sachs. Some American investment managers have used the U.S. affiliates to work their way into the Japanese web of connections. Or, if you independently win a securities firm as a distributor of a mutual fund, they can rope in other *keiretsu* members, like life or casualty insurance companies, as institutional clients.

Many American investment management firms have been "discovered" by Japanese firms on study tours. Groups like the Technology Transfer Institute run multi-city tours for representatives of assorted Japanese companies. The Japanese learned about the U.S. firms' strong points and gradually developed personal relationships with the portfolio managers and then hired the U.S. firms. But American managers who don't provide good service can't retain Japanese clients.

Retaining Your Japanese Client

Looking after the client is important. "American investment managers are like used-car salesmen," complains the New York representative of a Japanese institutional investor. How? "They are all over me when they want to sell something, just like a car salesman. But when I come back with a problem, they don't want to know me. This would never happen in Japan."

You may have to adjust your idea of service when dealing with the Japanese. While many American clients prefer a minimum of contact with their portfolio manager, Japanese like more frequent communication. Ideally you should have a Tokyo-based representative who will pay close attention to the account and coordinate regular visits from the U.S. parent company. Or hook up with a U.S. firm like Merrill Lynch or Citibank, which can represent you through their Tokyo office.

Translate your business cards and key documents into Japanese. Use a professional translator, but get a Japanese knowledgeable about investments to check their work. A persuasive document is not translated literally word for word. An American investment manager proposed a bridge fund to the Japanese. When he pitched his product in Tokyo, he discovered that his Japanese translation talked about "bridge" as in "Brooklyn Bridge" instead of as in "interim financing."

Keep your client well informed, particularly about sensitive issues. Since a lifetime commitment to one company is common in Japan, news of portfolio manager turnover upsets Japanese clients, especially if they hear about it first from the ex-manager. In Japan, a departing manager will often introduce his successor in person to his customers.

Pay attention to details. A conscientious fund accountant discovered that a Japanese client complained to a vice-president of her firm when her monthly report was off by $1.69. Her American clients wouldn't have even noticed. Now she keeps the Japanese happy.

Consider redesigning your statements. Japanese are easily confused by footnotes and cross-references to other pages. A simpler statement could spare you many frantic fax messages from Tokyo.

Be prepared for a different approach to performance. Though few American investment managers still use the Dow-Jones Industrial Average as their benchmark for U.S. stocks, many Japanese do. They've barely heard of the S&P 500, so don't be surprised if they blink with puzzlement when you suggest the Wilshire 2000 as the best benchmark. And the bottom line is that your client cares most about after-tax performance in yen without regard to American stock market activity.

Speaking of performance, the consultants who have made such a big deal of performance numbers in the United States barely exist in Japan. However, like you, they view Japan as a promising market. Firms like Frank Russell and InterSec are winning some clients. But Japanese clients are unlikely to deluge you with time-consuming consultant questionnaires and RFPs.

What Does It Mean?

American investment management firms with attractive investment performance records, experience in global investment markets, and advanced investment technology have the opportunity to obtain lucrative business from Japanese clients, particularly if they are willing to accommodate the Japanese in their approach to business development and management. To retain this business over the long term, American firms will have to offer good service and continue their advances in the development of new financial instruments and technology.

.

6

Enhancing the Fund Sponsor-Investment Manager Relationship

DAVID L. EAGER

*Managing Partner,
Eager & Associates*

It's time for a change. Plan sponsors and investment managers have a lot more to gain from each other than they currently do. There are numerous ways that each party can enhance the relationship. In the end, both the sponsor and the manager will come out winners.

Performance Expectations Must Become More Realistic

The change should begin with a reexamination of performance expectations by fund sponsors. To start, performance expectations must become more realistic. Since the early 1970s, sponsors have sought managers who "can consistently outperform the market . . . the SEI top quartile manager . . . in rising and falling markets . . . with below average risk." The constant search for stellar managers has been costly.

The continuous firing of "underperforming" managers may have collectively cost many funds more than the grand total of all their below-median performance. Each manager termination and the resulting reassignment of assets has a number of (hidden) costs. Consider Exhibit I—the cost of a change in managers for a $10 million portfolio: the fund sponsor's new manager would have to outperform the terminated manager by three percent just to pay for the change.

The futility of this constant reshuffling of managers is best depicted by one Southwestern corporate fund sponsor's dilemma. The vice-president of finance was conducting a search to replace an underperforming manager for his pension fund. His consultant presented an ideal candidate with a great five-year record. The dilemma? The sponsor had fired that manager five years

69

EXHIBIT I
Cost of a Change in Managers for a $10 million Portfolio

Cost	Possible Amount (as a % of assets)		
Market impact of purchases and sales in transitioning to the new manager's portfolio	1.0% per transaction x 2 (roundtrip)	=	2.00%
Brokerage to realign the portfolio	$.07/share x 2 divided by $40/share	=	.35%
Manager search consultant's fees	$20,000 divided by $10 million	=	.20%
Time and travel for sponsor's staff	$30,000 divided by $10 million	=	.30%
Legal, custody, and trustee fees	$15,000 divided by $10 million	=	.15%
Total Cost			3.00%

earlier for underperformance. Investment managers, too, need to shift their focus away from just performance. Often, investment managers fail to look beyond their own portion of a multimanager fund, and consequently, they fail to provide valuable advice and counsel.

Many funds would benefit if their fund sponsor and their investment manager(s) agreed upon two objectives:

- Reduce manager turnover—thereby reducing the cost of managing the fund; and

- Increase the manager's responsibility to communicate, service, and consult.

Currently, too much attention is paid to other ways to reduce fund costs. Managers' fees and brokerage have been the focus of cost reduction efforts. That's because they are visible targets, cost reduction is measurable, and many sponsors feel managers' services are overpriced. But constructive efforts to increase the value of investment managers' services and reduce the level of manager turnover can provide greater financial rewards to funds.

Here are ten rules to improve the relationship and help achieve the objectives of reducing manager turnover cost and increasing the value of investment managers' services. Many of the rules have been developed from the findings of over one thousand interviews with fund sponsors conducted by Eager & Associates.

Sponsors

RULE 1
Define reasonable and realistic investment performance goals.

Benchmarks should be well thought out. In a multimanager program, the sum of all of the individual goals should equal the overall goal.

If the performance expectations vary under differing market conditions, define them as such. For example, "during an extended period of rising interest rates, we expect the manager to earn at least the return of a seven-year Treasury (in the fixed income portfolio) with no more standard deviation of return than the Treasury."

Be explicit about the type of securities allowed and the extent to which you would expect the manager to over- or under-emphasize them.

RULE 2
Define your servicing, communications, and counseling requirements.

The results of Eager & Associates' client satisfaction surveys indicate that different sponsors have different communications preferences (see Exhibit II).

The best way to ensure that your managers tailor their servicing is to define your own specific requirements. Seek agreement within your organization regarding expectations. Define requirements in writing and insist that the manager(s) satisfy them. At least one consulting firm, Ennis, Knupp & Associates, wisely incorporates the manager's servicing and communications requirements in the fund sponsor's Statement of Investment Objectives. Others, including the Frank Russell Company, now review each manager's client servicing practices in their manager research efforts.

Sponsors also have a right to expect counseling and advice on matters of overall fund management. This is not meant to usurp the role of the consultants, but to strengthen the input. Nor should a manager be relied upon for judgement beyond their area of expertise or their fiduciary capacity.

EXHIBIT II
Servicing Preferences of Three Randomly Selected Fund Sponsors

	Sponsor A	*Sponsor B*	*Sponsor C*
Communications			
Personal meetings per year (one-on-one)	2–3	2	1
Phone calls discussing your needs per year	As needed	12	4
Periodic written updates (frequency)	2–3	4	12
Newsletters per year	Nice, but not necessary	Not interested	12
Preferred primary contact	Portfolio Mgr.	Chief Inv. Officer	Relationship Mgr.
Review Meetings			
Fund sponsor/inv. mgr. meetings per year	1	2	4
Who should initiate mtgs.	Sponsor	Investment Mgr.	Consultant
Preferred meeting location	Manager	Sponsor	Alternate
Who should attend	Portfolio Mgr.	Chief Inv. Officer Relationship Mgr.	Portfolio Mgr. Sr. Inv. Officer Relationship Mgr.
Meeting length	30 minutes	Over 1 hour	45 min. – 1 hour

RULE 3
Develop a thorough due diligence process to be used in each new appointment of an investment manager.

The process should focus on answering two questions:

• Does the manager have a high likelihood of achieving our investment return objectives?

• Will they satisfy our servicing, communications, and counseling requirements?

A well-run investment management organization should have

• defined their own beliefs (philosophy) about investments, the markets, and how they should manage assets;

• an organizational structure and decision-making process that links directly to their beliefs; and

• a process to continually review and evaluate their investment process to assure it is appropriate for current and foreseeable conditions.

Sponsors should examine the logic and linkage of how the manager presents their beliefs (philosophy), organization, investment approach, and management controls.

Performance should be fully scrutinized. Fund sponsors should gather data from every source available, including mutual funds or commingled funds managed by the investment firm, 13-F filing reports, other fund sponsors who use that manager, and your consultant's performance report on the manager. Ask your consultant for the actual performance the manager has had with their clients (on an anonymous basis). Be able to compare and fully explain any apparent discrepancies.

Satisfying the "client servicing" test requires far more than having the fund sponsor's selection committee hear a finals presentation from the manager. Start by reviewing your own servicing expectations. How closely does the manager come to fitting your requirements? Ask for references, then *talk* with them. Focus your inquiries on servicing, communications, and counseling. Finally, ask the manager to provide copies of all types of communications.

RULE 4
Take a pro-active role in the relationship with your investment manager.

Begin by making sure they clearly understand why they were hired. Discuss any concerns that existed at the time of hiring. Allow the manager to address those concerns.

The ongoing interaction between the fund sponsor and the investment manager needs to become more of a *team effort* aimed at achieving common goals. Unfortunately, the relationship between a fund sponsor and its manager is frequently different than the sponsor's relationship with their accountants, outside attorneys, or other outside professionals providing advice. *The sponsor-manager relationship is often based upon the sponsor's skepticism and the manager's defensiveness.* It focuses too much on the past and not enough on the future. It is short term oriented. And it's not collaborative.

Review meetings should have an agenda that has joint responsibilities. The agenda should focus on the past *and* the future. The sponsor should provide insight into issues that affect the overall plan as well as the specific manager's assignment. Funding and cash flow projections and requirements should be provided continually. And, the anticipated placement or source of cash flows should be discussed openly.

Meet at the investment manager's location regularly. Attend their internal meetings to keep your level of understanding of their firm and their staffing current.

RULE 5
Don't over-diversify your stable of managers.

It's not uncommon today for a fund sponsor to employ dozens of investment managers. It's not always necessary, and over-diversification increases both the sponsor's costs *and* the time commitment to overseeing the fund (and its managers).

If fund sponsors are going to improve the way they work with their managers, they must make more time available to work with each manager. For some sponsors, that may mean a reduction in managers, especially if their rosters look like a mini *Money Market Directory.*

Investment Managers

RULE 1
Know why you were hired and what is specifically expected of you.

One of the single greatest failings of investment managers is accepting accounts with investment objectives that are not reasonable for their firm. The temptation exists to accept an inappropriate goal *simply to land a new account.*

Managers must have disciplines that overrule this new-business "temptation." They should take the initiative to work out investment goals that are compatible and realistic. And, they should decline to take on assignments where agreement cannot be reached.

Make sure you know the rationale behind your hiring and the sponsor's expectations of you, including performance evaluation benchmarks, time frame, portfolio guidelines and restrictions, and style expectations. It's best to settle disagreements up front—before the relationship has officially been launched.

RULE 2
Profile your client's servicing, communications, and counseling needs.

If your client hasn't defined this already, get agreement from them in writing. The profile should define

- required written communication, content, frequency, and due dates;

- meeting preferences, including frequency, location, agenda, attendees, and roles; and

- areas where the client would expect other counsel.

The profile should be provided to everyone in the investment firm who has interaction with or is involved in the servicing of the client.

Tailor your servicing, communication, and counsel according to the profile. The profile serves as your guide. Compliance with it should be monitored internally. By better organizing and defining your clients' servicing requirements, support staff can begin to take more of the responsibility off of portfolio managers' shoulders.

RULE 3
Make sure your client is knowledgeable of all your investment products.

Oftentimes, opportunities are missed to attract additional assets from your own clients. There are several steps you can take to ensure that your clients are knowledgeable of all your products:

- Discuss your client's needs—both current and future—and relate your products to those needs;

- Provide marketing materials on all products;

- Present different products periodically in a meeting separate from the quarterly performance review; and

- Develop quarterly newsletters that feature a different product in each issue.

Encourage your clients to visit your offices. That will give them the opportunity to meet investment people other than their portfolio manager, and provides broader exposure of your firm.

RULE 4
Understand your client's total investment program.

It's the only way you can successfully fill your role as a manager and advisor to your clients. Becoming more involved with your clients can pay big dividends. You should always keep on top of other "roles" you may fill (in the manager's roster) by keeping the sponsor abreast of your firm's *total* capabilities.

When interviewed by Eager & Associates, sponsors typically express the same concern about multiproduct managers. They say the managers generally don't do a good job of explaining their other capabilities. In fact, when sponsors are asked to name other products offered by their managers, only about fifty percent can specifically name any of their managers' other products. And, of those who can name a product, less than half have a high-enough level of understanding to be able to explain the product to others. The moral of the story: helping your client satisfy an investment need with one of *your* investment products is good business for both of you. But they must be aware of your products in order to use them.

RULE 5
Survey your clients for feedback.

Every twelve to twenty-four months clients should be surveyed or interviewed to test

* their level of satisfaction with your firm;

* important factors in their relationship with you; and

* their current preferences for communications and servicing.

The survey and/or interviews should be systematic, uniform, and conducted by someone other than the portfolio manager or account manager.

The feedback allows your firm to address organizational weaknesses and to adjust specific client servicing preferences as they change. Small problems can be corrected before they become large problems. And, it keeps everyone on their toes with regard to servicing.

In conclusion, the relationship between fund sponsors and investment managers can produce a great deal more value than it has previously. To do so requires that sponsors demand—and managers provide—far more than just portfolio returns.

Marketing Mutual Funds to Defined Contribution Plans

CURTIS VOSTI

Reporter,
Pensions & Investments

The mutual fund industry faces a period of intense competition in the 1990s following a decade of extraordinary growth.

Between 1980 and 1991, the number of mutual funds grew to more than 1,000 from about 250. In assets under management, the funds now control more than $1 trillion, up from just $100 billion at the beginning of 1980.

But the twenty percent annual growth in the 1980s has resulted in increased competition in the 1990s, just when the rate of asset growth is expected to slow to ten percent to fifteen percent per annum.

The competition is coming from banks, investment management firms that have not emphasized mutual funds in the past, brokerage firms offering "wrap fee" programs, and large corporations offering in-house mutual fund manager of managers-style investment management to their employees, pension beneficiaries, and even to outside clients.

How well armed the mutual fund industry is to defend its turf remains to be seen. Thoughtful people in the industry, however, are not taking the challenge lightly.

"The mutual fund industry is going to be open game for any financial service company in the 1990s," said John Bogle, chairman of the board of the Vanguard Group of Cos.

"The easy wins are behind us for our industry," said Charles Salisbury, managing director of T. Rowe Price. "Now we'll start to see who the real winners are going to be."

The challengers also face some daunting hurdles.

"The business isn't just investment management anymore," said Bob Reynolds, president of Fidelity Institutional Services Inc. "It is providing record keeping and other services."

"The shape of and access to the distribution system are the make-or-break issues for the 1990s," said a report by the Investment Company Institute, a Washington-based mutual fund trade group.

Distribution patterns will shift a great deal in the coming decade, said A. Michael Lipper, president of Lipper Analytic Services Inc. Banks, insurance companies, and brokerage firms all will compete with traditional mutual fund companies, he said. According to Exhibit 1, marketing will become even more important as distribution channels increase.

EXHIBIT 1 Mutual Fund Direct Marketers*

1989

Deposit Institutions	19%
Discount Brokers	1
Direct Sales	65
In-house Management	15

1990

Deposit Institutions	19%
Discount Brokers	1
Direct Sales	63
In-house Management	16
Other	1

1995

Deposit Institutions	21%
Discount Brokers	1
Direct Sales	54
In-house Management	18
Other	4

*Sales by channel; 1995 projected.
Source: Investment Company Institute, Washington

The Sincerest Form of Flattery

In effect, the success of mutual funds in the 1980s has caused competitors to emulate them.

In addition, in the coming decade, traditional mutual fund companies like Fidelity, Vanguard, and T. Rowe Price will be challenged not only by a host of new players, but also by pressures on costs, supply, and marketing.

Mutual funds, which have faced and conquered adversity in the past, will not surrender easily before the challenges.

In the 1960s, mutual funds enjoyed a brief surge in popularity with the "Nifty 50" stock funds. But the go-go years proved short-lived, and investors soon found the value of their holdings cut in half as the markets plunged in the 1970s.

In the early 1970s, redemptions of mutual fund shares outpaced sales, and the industry's future looked dim.

A rebound occurred, thanks to the development of money market funds, which combined the pooled fund attractions of the funds with the high interest rates of the period.

In effect, the industry used innovation to make itself competitive and extend the life of its product. In the process, it put itself into competition with banks and took part of the banks' traditional source of funds—passbook savers.

"It was hard to go to a party without people talking about how their mutual fund money markets were doing," recalled Robert Rudell, vice president for institutional marketing for IDS Financial Services Inc. "It was hot stuff, and brought in a lot of customers."

But the drop in rates in the early 1980s caused the industry to reassess itself. It broadened its horizons with the introduction of bond funds and high-yield vehicles, but again, after a spell, those found themselves out of favor.

The real growth of the 1980s was sparked by the short-lived tax advantages for individual retirement accounts and the spurt of assets going into 401(k) salary reduction plans after 1982.

Now, as the industry moves into the 1990s, the ability to recreate itself through innovative product offerings will take a back seat to other abilities—those of participant education, administration, and distribution.

And although the market will be growing more slowly than in the heady 1980s, it still will be a market worth fighting for.

Household discretionary income is projected to rise to $16.2 trillion in the year 2000, up from $10.3 trillion in 1995 and $6.7 trillion in 1990.

Mutual funds are expected to get 17.6 percent of that discretionary income in 2000, up from 15.5 percent in 1995 and 14.5 percent in 1990.

One reason for the explosive growth of mutual funds is the increasing use of defined contribution plans by sponsors.

Defined Contribution Opportunities

In 1797, Albert Gallatin, soon thereafter to be Secretary of Treasury under presidents Jefferson and Madison, began what is said to be the nation's first defined contribution plan at his Gallatin Glass Works in New Geneva, Pennsylvania.

His idea was to give employees half of the firm's profits. "The democratic principle upon which our nation was founded should not be restricted to the political processes, but should be applied to the industrial process as well," Mr. Gallatin said.

Now, 194 years later, those democratic principles have been handed down to a descendant of Mr. Gallatin's profit-sharing plan—the 401(k) salary reduction plan.

As the most popular defined contribution plans, 401(k)s have tripled their participation rate between 1975 and 1987, the most recent year for which the General Accounting Office has compiled figures.

But with the popularity comes a host of potential problems. As managers, record keepers, and consultants rush in to service the fast-growing field, some find the grass isn't as green as it appears.

The challenge of educating plan participants is critical. However, it is unclear at this point whether the education process will be the province of sponsors, the government, or, through marketing, the responsibility of the mutual fund provider.

While not as large as defined benefit plans, defined contribution plans in their many forms—profit-sharing, thrift/savings, deferred cash, employee stock ownership, and, most recently, 401(k) or salary reduction plans— have grown in recent years to become the focal point of employee benefit activity.

According to Greenwich Associates, total defined contribution assets grew to $289 billion in 1990 from $224 billion in 1988. Assets in stand-alone 401(k) plans grew to $89 billion in 1990 from $71 billion in 1988. Additionally, $139 billion were in hybrid defined contribution plans, many of which have 401(k) features.

The plans have grabbed the attention and imagination of sponsors, the investment community, consultants, and, most importantly, plan participants. As these concepts have matured, the players have become more sophisticated and plan participants more demanding. They realize they have a direct and visible stake in their account balance sheet most receive every month.

But while participants gravitate toward these plans, providers have started a stampede.

As it became apparent in the mid-1980s that 401(k) and other defined contribution plans were here to stay, a bevy of investment managers, mutual funds, insurance companies, consultants, and banks turned their energies toward capturing a share of the marketplace.

"At the time it was introduced, 401(k) was the backwater of the employee benefits area. It was not considered terribly important," said one mutual fund representative.

But as more firms entered the field, the huge start-up costs and the growing demand for easy, comprehensive services proved to be too much for some of the players.

"A number of banks got involved because it looked like a good way to provide total services to their clients," said Hal Hopkins, vice president of Prudential Asset Management Co. "But some have dropped it as it became apparent that it is more complicated than anything they've ever seen.

"There is a significant saturation of players, and there's been a shakeout taking place for the last year or so."

Mutual funds, with their built-in, client-responsive services, have made great inroads into the servicing and availability of investment options for plan participants. Insurance companies, with their popular guaranteed contracts, remain a dominant player. Money management firms, which traditionally have focused on separate accounts and commingled funds, now are plotting to grab their share.

Consultants, who had to shift gears to serve the market, soon found that the discrimination testing requirements of defined contribution plans occupied most of their attention. "There has been so much compliance testing, there have been times when benefit design was put on hold," said Richard Koski, benefits consultant at Buck Pension Fund Services.

Soup to Nuts Services

As sponsors of defined contribution plans expand to better serve participants, they run into the question, "How much is enough?"

Marketing professionals are learning that not only must they communicate performance, they must also stress features unheard of in the defined benefit realm.

According to a 1990 survey by Hewitt Associates, seventy-six percent of 401(k) plans allow asset transfers on a quarterly or more frequent basis. Another 1990 study, by Greenwich Associates, reported ninety-five percent of its surveyed defined contribution plans allowed transfers at least quarterly. Hewitt reported twelve percent allow daily transfers; Greenwich, fourteen percent.

But the move toward more frequent, in many cases daily, transfers is now being questioned by some providers and plan sponsors. Some consider imposing fees or other limitations on the number of transfers allowed, wondering if participants need to be able to juggle their assets on a daily basis and if the plan's needs are best met through daily valuations.

As 401(k) plans grow, expand, and face the salient issues surrounding retirement benefits, the keys to plan participants' well-being need to be identified, according to James Hiner, principal at William M. Mercer, Inc.

"We see a major shift of responsibility being passed on to the participant for retirement planning," he said. "Communicating the best way to do that is a real challenge."

Merely educating the plan participant on the benefits of various investments is a tough job. "Some people are risk averse no matter what the level of education." If GICs had not been invented, Mr. Hiner said, participants likely would put their assets into money market funds, which return even less.

Plan sponsors seeking to help the participant get pertinent information on expected risks and returns of various investments face a tricky situation, Mr. Hiner said. They have to provide enough information to help participants make good decisions, but not too much to assume fiduciary liability for those individual decisions.

Despite growing pains, it is likely that 401(k) plans will continue to grow in the 1990s.

Competing for the Business

The major mutual fund companies find themselves in a good position to fight the challengers. The strengths that allowed Fidelity, Vanguard, and T. Rowe Price to dominate during the growth decade—their "brand name" products readily identifiable to all potential customers, their marketing skills, and their customer-pleasing administrative services—will stand them in good stead in the slower growth of the 1990s.

But the new competitors have learned what made the Big Three successful; now they're attempting to emulate them. And each type of competitor has some advantages of its own.

President Bush's banking reform proposal has urged liberalization of the banking industry's role in marketing, distributing, and managing mutual funds. Banks have large customer bases, and those customers are in contact with the banks almost on a daily basis. The major banks also have well-developed marketing departments and powerful computer networks that could allow them to provide the necessary administrative services.

"Everybody's looking for the banking system to play a larger role," said Frank Sebestyen, senior vice president for State Street Bank & Trust Co.

Brokerage firms offering "wrap fee" accounts also pose a threat. That type of account appears to offer the sophisticated customer more personal attention than he or she can get from mutual funds.

For the wrap fee, the customer gets the advice and hand holding of a broker-consultant and the management expertise of one or more top investment management firms. And the brokerage firms have large customer bases, large numbers of registered representatives telephoning and knocking on doors to sell the product, and large computer systems on which to mount improved administrative packages.

"The challenge for the fund industry is to make sure the mutual funds are inside most of the wrappers," the Investment Company Institute report said, referring to the opportunity for the industry to provide its services to brokerages.

In addition, large corporations are offering their own "private label" mutual fund products to their employees and others.

Concerned about their employees' retirement savings, several large plan sponsors—including Bell Atlantic

Corp., IBM Corp., Owens-Illinois Inc., Bechtel Power Corp., State Farm Insurance Cos., General Electric Co., Caterpillar Inc., and American Airlines Inc.—have created their own mutual funds.

The Big Get Bigger

The one area where little new competition is expected is the mutual fund industry itself. Few start-up niche funds are in the cards.

The Investment Company Institute report noted that with all the product innovation of the 1980s, it will be hard for new niche players to emerge. But William G. Waller, senior vice president of the Strong Funds, part of Strong/Corneliuson Capital Management Inc., said the industry needs the new blood.

"If there ever was an industry crying out for new people, it is the mutual fund industry," he said. "However, it's tough to build a name."

Jon Fossell, chairman of Oppenheimer Management Corp. said economies of scale provide a big barrier to new entrants. "Unless you have a couple of billion (dollars) under management, you don't break even."

But Mr. Lipper cautions against ruling out the entrepreneurial spirit that nurtured the mutual fund industry through the growing years.

"It's a very creative industry," he said. "Don't think of niche in terms of portfolios. The mutual fund industry is fundamentally a marketing business. Out of that will come some talent that will make it."

There are several ways the mutual industry can counter the competition it will receive from banks, brokers, and corporations.

First, it can (and already does to some extent) sell wholesale its products to banks and even brokerage houses for them to retail.

Fidelity's Mr. Reynolds said mutual fund companies like Fidelity can work with banks, providing help in a number of service areas that have stymied some of the early banking efforts in the field.

While some major banks probably will start their own mutual funds or buy existing ones if the Glass-Steagall Act is abolished, many smaller banks undoubtedly will find retailing existing funds attractive compared with the costs of starting or buying their own families.

Second, mutual funds can build on what seems to be a technological advantage on the administrative side to stay ahead of the competition.

According to Michael Hines, vice president of marketing development for Fidelity, in the 1990s the emphasis will switch to service from products. "The product was the story of the 1980s," he said. "Much of what you are going to see out there (in terms of product) five years from now is already out there."

As the emphasis switches to service, Mr. Hines said, the mutual funds have "hidden technologies" that help to organize what can become a complicated system of investment, record keeping, education, and information. "It can become fairly complicated very easily," he said.

Explaining the complicated features of mutual funds to individual investors will become a key to the success of mutual fund providers, experts agree. In this effort, tools of the retail marketing process—advertising, public relations, materials, etc.—will play a crucial role. In the battle to gain market share, these tools will be more important in defined contribution marketing than they are in defined benefit marketing.

While the market is growing more slowly, and competition is intensifying, there still are great opportunities for the top mutual fund organizations.

According to the Investment Company Institute, individuals investing through corporate retirement plans— the "insti-vidual market"—are the most promising source of new assets for the mutual fund industry.

Through the popular participant-directed retirement vehicles, mutual funds will be able to get their foot in the door for personal savings and retirement roll-overs.

"Mutual funds have become an important linchpin of personal financial planning: capital accumulation, retirement planning, medical care, saving for tuition, etc.," IDS's Mr. Rudell said.

"Increasingly, funds will not be sold on their features nor intended customer but rather on the goals they help to fulfill," the Investment Company Institute's report concluded.

Changing demographics also are expected to play a role in the continued popularity of mutual fund investing and the changing nature of the business. Two-wage-earner families are becoming the norm, and Fidelity's Mr. Hines said although there was a decline in the savings rate among individuals between 1980 and 1991, the pool of new savings investment continues to be large. "Even with a recession on, there are so many dual wage-earning families, there are tremendous amounts of savings," he said. While not everyone agrees savings rates will climb in the coming decade, Mr. Hines said, either way it doesn't matter. In January 1980, with a personal savings rate of 6.48 percent, new savings grew by $119 billion; in January 1991, with a savings rate of just 4.68 percent, new savings still grew by $187.4 billion. In

January 1989, new savings stood at $157 billion. "There is a tendency toward higher savings," he said. "United States investors are trying to get their financial houses in order."

Mutual funds are likely to benefit from changing savings patterns and from preliminary signs of an increase in the money supply, Mr. Lipper said.

"There will be a societal shift to savings and investments," he said. "If inflation does not rear its ugly head, (an increasing money supply) could last long enough to be a real shot in the arm to investment flows.

"It used to be that the home was the biggest investment (for an individual), and it always used to go up in value. Now, home values don't always go up. It's no longer a safe bet to sell your home for a sufficient enough profit."

Convincing dual wage-earners, many of whom were reared on television advertising, to invest in one mutual fund or another will call for specialized and effective marketing efforts. Some in the industry feel that equity mutual funds may have the best shot at increasing market share.

"A bold assumption might be that fixed income (funds) will drop to sixty-five percent from seventy-five percent," Mr. Lipper said. "If you add ten percent to equity, that's a forty-percent increase for the decade."

Indeed, the Investment Company Institute believes many forces are at work to bring equity funds back to center stage.

Corporate efforts to "re-equify" after years of debt, customers' realization that they need the higher long-term returns of equities to finance retirement and other expenses, and the margin squeeze on managers all will help focus on equity products.

"The successful product will combine equity-like returns with comfort for the risk averse," the Investment Company Institute report said. "Equity managers with proven (track) records will be at a premium." Quantitative techniques and indexing also will play increasing roles, as the pressures of cost containment add to the shortage of equity managers, the report added.

"The pressure to allow these techniques into the individual marketplace through mutual funds is bound to increase, especially if the markets remain volatile," the report said.

Meanwhile, Mary Barneby, former president of the benefits division of Dreyfus Group Retirement Plans, said there still will be room for the funds that show stellar returns. "Good performance is always noticed," she said. "There's still room for good managers."

And good performance will attract investment dollars to the mutual fund industry in the 1990s.

So weep not for the mutual fund industry in the slow-growth 1990s. With the aid of sophisticated marketing, it is well positioned to meet the emerging competition head on and to defend its turf.

This chapter is adapted from articles appearing in the May 13, 1991 and April 1, 1991 issues of *Pensions & Investments.*

8

Marketing Small, Emerging, and Minority-Owned Investment Firms

AMIE DIXON STAMBERG

President,
Stamberg Prestia Ltd.

Small, emerging, and minority-owned firms have unique characteristics, usually preconceived as negatives, that must be addressed in the marketing process. These can include short in-house performance history, small, little or no institutional assets under management, a "one-man shop," recent establishment of the organization, lack of experience in dealing with consultants and institutional staff/trustees, a limited staff and budget for marketing, and an undiversified product line.

Many of these issues, if handled properly through the marketing process, can be turned into positives relatively quickly, and, with the passage of some time, all can be repositioned as positives for your firm.

All marketing advice regarding the investment side of the business for larger firms pertains to smaller firms as well. This chapter will concentrate on the unique barriers and challenges to marketing emerging and minority-owned firms, as well as the advantages that those smaller firms have.

For example, one need not spend much time dealing with organizational charts, committee structures, and cumbersome decision-making processes within an emerging firm. The question of how the research analysts communicate with the portfolio managers rarely comes up since, in a small firm, they are usually the same people. Communication and speed of implementing ideas can be much more effective within a smaller investment company, and this is an advantage that the marketing staff should emphasize.

Overall, emerging and minority-owned firms generally do not yet have an established credibility and visibility in the marketplace. The organization does not have a personality of its own; rather, it is closely intertwined with that of the founder and key principal(s). The obvious exception occurs when very well-known figures, such as Peter Lynch or Warren Buffet, leave their former organization to start up their own business. Unfortunately, most of us do not have the luxury of marketing a household name when we are representing an emerging or smaller firm.

The ingredients of attaining visibility and credibility include the manager's experience in the field and track record with prior affiliations; current and former clientele; reputation for delivering a high-quality product; reputation for flawless operations; placing the firm into every consultant database possible and keeping that up-to-date; calling on funds with whom the principals or marketer already have a relationship; cold calls; reputation for quality research; publicity; and an organization that is constructed to focus on and deliver excellence in the product offered.

The trick is, how does one use the limited financial and human resources of a smaller firm to accomplish all of the above without sacrificing any standards of quality or performance in the investment product itself?

Usually, start-up is the hardest hurdle to overcome. All the comments in this chapter pertain to the start-up phase of a company too, but the time frames are likely to be much longer. The critical aspects of a start-up firm are having enough money to weather the first two to three years, having an "angel" or seed account that allows one to begin to develop an internal track record immediately, an ability to accept large amounts of rejection, and a tenacity to keep plugging away with a strong belief in one's product and process.

Those emerging and minority-owned firms who have already accomplished this first phase are well ahead, and strongly positioned to be more successful. Success depends on a strong business plan, a strong marketing plan, a feverish adherence to your investment philosophy, consistent implementation of the investment approach, and a well-set-up back office. Favorable market cycles and a lot of luck don't hurt. The venture capital/start-up phase can take anywhere from six months to five years depending on the above variables. Having commented about the start-up phase of investment firms, the case study firm, Avalon Capital, has gone through start-up and is in a credible position to really start a national marketing campaign and to incur those costs. Results can be expected within three years, or with some luck, a bit sooner.

Don't Even Bother to Think About a Marketing Program Unless You Are Willing to Give It a Three-Year Time Horizon

The mistake that most investment managers make is to assume that their good performance record will enable money to fall in over the transom if they just go out and hire a marketing person. Forget it. The manager will be frustrated and the marketeer will be frustrated and it will be a waste of money. The only way a marketing program can work is if both the investment professionals and the marketing professionals work closely together and have a mutual respect and understanding for each other's talents and skills.

MARKETING AN EMERGING FIRM: A CASE STUDY

I have given our case study some reasonable credentials. Still, the average institutional pension fund would not touch Avalon at this point in time. This firm is exemplary of the sort of small, emerging, or minority-owned firm that could grow to the $300 to 500 million level within the next three years, given a good product, performance, and marketing. This firm has made it through the first venture capital/start-up hurdle, and does have a few years of experience as an entity with several decent clients.

Avalon Capital Management is a fictional two-year-old investment management company which has $75 million under management in six accounts. One account is a well-known institution. For a minority firm, the scenario could be much the same, but the institutional client would more likely be a public fund.

The firm is one-hundred percent employee owned and has one lead portfolio manager, two middle-level research analysts (the portfolio manager is a senior research analyst as well), a trader who also handles the administration of the firm, and a secretary. At an average fifty basis point fee, the firm generates nearly $400,000 in revenues, which is adequate to cover the cost of doing business and to pay a modest salary to the owners. The senior partner has ten years of prior portfolio management experience at a well-known company. Through savings, investment, or private backing, the firm has working capital to stay in business another three years without getting a new account.

Avalon Capital manages large-cap, value equity portfolios, with the capability of running balanced accounts for individuals, which account for fifty percent of their assets. They do not want to develop an institutional fixed income product now, but could in the future if their assets grow larger and they hire a fixed income manager. Now, they would like to concentrate on growing their institutional base of value-equity clients to twenty-five accounts representing about $500 million. Staff might be added at the research level and an analyst could be promoted to portfolio manager as account numbers grow. Basically, they are staffed to grow and their performance has been in the second quartile for the last two years. The last two years have not been particularly kind to value managers, so Avalon looks very good against their peer groups. When value comes back into favor, they want the marketing program already established so they are positioned to capitalize on it.

Avalon Capital knows this marketing goal could take five years to accomplish, but they feel it is reasonable, especially with a more favorable market, to obtain this kind of growth within three years.

The partners at Avalon do not have any direct marketing experience per se, and prefer to hire somebody to do the marketing and to have that person be the lead on client servicing. This way the investment partners can concentrate on running money, and become involved in presentations only when there is a high level of interest.

SELECTING A MARKETING PERSON

Avalon Capital has investigated two options: hiring an experienced marketing person to work full time for Avalon Capital, and hiring a marketing representative who represents several noncompeting firms simultaneously.

Avalon found several individuals who were well qualified to work in-house. The advantages are that the marketer would be in-house full time: working only for Avalon Capital, he/she could grow with the firm and establish a very close relationship with the investment professionals and clients. The marketing person could train and grow the marketing staff, if and when Avalon decided to expand its product line in the future. The disadvantages, as Avalon saw it, of hiring an in-house marketing person included the fact that they had never worked with this person before. That unknown was of concern because Avalon's existing team worked very well together. They did not want to jeopardize that mix in any way. The salary demanded was $150,000 a year, quite average for a well-experienced, proven institutional marketing person, plus a guaranteed bonus and/or a percentage of the management fees brought in, benefits, office, and secretary. Estimated travel and entertainment expenses were $75,000 to $125,000 a year, depending upon the target market.

In considering an outside firm or marketing representative, Avalon concluded that the positive side included a much lower cost ($50,000 to $75,000 annual retainer plus twenty percent of the management fees). The representative paid all business expenses and shared travel and entertainment expenses with Avalon. The representative had experience in launching emerging and minority-owned firms into successful organizations; the representative would limit its client base to three and would work like a partner, but without having a claim to stock in Avalon. The representative's contract ran two years and was renewable as is for another two years.

Both the in-house marketing person and the marketing representative would perform essentially the same duties. For a variety of reasons, financial and organizational, Avalon felt that the marketing representative was a better way for them to go at this juncture. Down the road, if they felt in-house personnel were needed for marketing, the marketing firm had agreed to identify and train an in-house staff for them. The marketing representative had experience marketing smaller and minority-owned firms. Since she had a woman-owned firm herself, Avalon felt that it might give them entree to some additional searches, and they had been considering a minority-owned joint venture with colleagues from their prior firm some time in the future.

ESTABLISHING AND IMPLEMENTING A MARKETING STRATEGY—YEAR ONE

In selecting a marketer, Avalon wanted someone or a firm experienced in the institutional marketing arena so they could hit the pavement running. The professionals at Avalon were not particularly familiar with the consultants, nor the current institutional marketplace, since they had not had much contact with those people at their prior firm. The marketing representative hired, Maria James, began by spending a full week in the offices of Avalon Capital, interviewing all of the professionals, reading up on the client's individual objectives, and becoming familiar with the portfolio characteristics and decision making behind the purchase and sale of portfolio holdings.

While familiarizing herself with the performance composite and helping Avalon to reconstruct it to conform to the standards required by most consultants and institutions, Maria set about organizing all of the data required for consultant questionnaires. She and Avalon worked together to compute the assets under management broken down by type of client, asset class, taxable/tax-free, personnel background, biographies, past portfolio characteristics, cash holdings, and current performance reports. After going through Avalon's record at their prior affiliation, they decided that it would be pertinent to display that too, as an historical performance record, since the senior investor at Avalon had been the sole portfolio manager on the accounts at the prior firm for the last five years.

Maria pointed out that, initially, the senior professional at Avalon would have to spend a lot of time with her, or any other marketing person, bringing her up to speed on the firm and helping her to organize and understand the information and process at Avalon. After that, Maria was able to proceed pretty much on her own, "parroting" the investment process, answering questions as the investment professionals would, and drawing on the portfolio manager only for specific questions, updates, and scheduling appointments which she had screened for a high level of interest.

Maria had developed a consultant and prospect list over her fifteen years in the marketing and consulting industry, and it included many people with whom she had developed a close professional relationship over the years. She broke down the consultants by primary and secondary priority, making a judgment as to which consultants would be more receptive and important to Avalon at this point in their life cycle. This became a key part of the marketing strategy.

During the first year, Avalon's target was to be in fifteen consultant data bases; for Maria to visit each of those consultants and familiarize them with Avalon after marketing and presentation materials had been developed; and to target certain public funds, corporations, and endowments with whom Avalon or Maria had an existing relationship. In marketing a small company, Maria had felt that the consultants provided her, as a marketing person, with the greatest leverage, and about seventy percent of the business she had targeted for Avalon would come from a consultant source initially. Maria also called her contacts at various magazines and industry publications to try to generate some publicity for Avalon, their product line, and new marketing effort.

After six months, Avalon had a two-and-one-half year track record that was in line with the S&P 500, their bogey, and first quartile performance compared with the value peer group universes. Maria had arranged to have several different vendors plot performance and portfolio characteristics on their universes for Avalon, and she would use that consultant's graph during presentations to the consultant or their clients.

DEVELOPING MARKETING MATERIALS

Avalon concurred that there was no point in starting a marketing campaign without having done their homework. For the first several months, all the marketing effort was spent internally organizing performance, assets, ADV's, biographies, and other information that would be required during meetings.

Maria had explained, and Avalon agreed, that marketing to institutions was exceedingly competitive, and that it was very hard to get an appointment with consultants or plan sponsors. Avalon only had one chance to make a good impression, and Maria recommended that they not use that bullet until they were ready to make a top-notch presentation. Therefore, she recommended that the next couple of months be devoted to developing a marketing booklet and a final presentation booklet, and to practicing the presentation extensively. In that way, they would be prepared and professional when they did begin to present to consultants and prospective clients face to face.

Maria suggested that Avalon hire a firm which specialized in developing brochures. While she felt that she and Avalon could easily write the text, the objectivity and the artistic and graphics capability of a specialty company that had a broad viewpoint and experience in developing marketing booklets would be a good investment. The cost ran between $10,000 and $50,000, depending on the amount of work and the type of brochure desired. Avalon decided to go with a lower-priced package, in which the marketing consultant would rough out the presentation booklet, and then Avalon and Maria would polish it and produce it. This involved a one-day workshop with the consultant identifying the key issues of Avalon to be emphasized, strengths and weaknesses of the firm to be dealt with, and how to display performance in the strongest contexts.

A distinction was made between a one-page profile, which would be sent out to interested parties; a marketing booklet containing more background information, which would be sent out to interested prospects; and the presentation booklet itself. In developing the marketing booklet themselves, Avalon Capital and Maria decided to select those features of consultant questionnaires that they thought were particularly informative and to combine them into a booklet that presented the background of the organization, investment philosophy, investment approach, biographies, assets, and a performance display. From the marketing booklet, they drew up a one-page "fact sheet" that could be accompanied by prospect letters. The fact sheet can change quarterly or semi-annually, depending on the progress of the firm, its performance, new accounts, etc.

The marketing booklet was designed to be used with consultants and clients who wanted comprehensive background on Avalon, and by Maria in introductory meetings with consultants and prospects of Avalon Capital.

Avalon's first-year goal was to meet and get on line with fifteen consultants and all their branch offices, be included in three final presentations, and land one account. The secondary goal was to plant many seeds of opportunity that would bloom during Years Two and Three.

MARKETING STRATEGY—YEAR TWO

By this time, Avalon Capital had continued to do well and now had a three-year performance record of its own, as well as the five-year record of the senior professional prior to forming Avalon. Many consultants were familiar with the company, and a few had even placed Avalon in finals for a value-oriented manager or part of a farm team. Avalon did win one of these finals, a $10-million account, and felt that the second year of marketing should emphasize improving the close ratio, addressing some of the issues which were perceived as negatives in the marketing efforts of the first year, and increasing their exposure to the institutional marketplace.

"Negatives" of Avalon in the marketplace included the following.

1. Avalon has only three years in business, with assets totalling $95 million in seven accounts.

   Avalon addresses this by pointing to the prior relevant, legitimate investment experience of the professional, totalling an eight-year track record, and adds that the small assets indicate a lot of capacity for new accounts.

2. Avalon only has one senior investment professional.

   Avalon emphasizes that they have beefed up the staff in anticipation of asset growth, adding that there is tremendous backup through their analysts and through Street research. In the "What if the portfolio manager gets hit by a beer truck?" scenario, there are knowledgable analysts to take over. Future plans include promoting one to portfolio manager responsibilities. Additionally, Avalon's large cap, value-oriented portfolio is extremely marketable. A client wishing to terminate Avalon because of personnel turnover would have no trouble liquidating the portfolio.

3. Avalon's numbers have been better than that of other value-oriented managers, but not much better than the market in general over the last three years.

   Avalon points to the fact that value-oriented styles have not been in favor the last few years, but over their historical performance, including a prior affiliation, they have proven to be first-quartile managers. Also, their style is very risk averse, and they add a tremendous value when the market is flat or down, but hope to stay up with the averages when the market is in a strong bull phase, as it is now. Compounding positive rates of return is very powerful, so Avalon stresses preservation of capital and limiting downside risk.

Maria and Avalon thought that they could close more business and be in more finals this year due to the efforts of marketing in Year One, increased length of their performance history, and by improving the final presentation and presentation booklet.

In redoing the presentation booklet, Avalon concentrated on creating short bullet statements on each page designed to make a specific point. That way the presentation could be anywhere from fifteen minutes to one hour using the same booklet. In the past, they had had trouble running over time limits, usually preset at thirty minutes or so, and in some cases had been unable to finish their presentation.

The first page of the booklet addressed the investment philosophy, phrased as "We invest in large-cap, value stocks to achieve high reward, low risk." Scatter diagrams and cumulative bar charts were bought to display the low-risk, high-reward features of the firm.

The second page addressed the organization by stating that "We are exceptionally well organized to invest institutional assets" and then a list of reasons, such as "outstanding academic and investment credentials, depth and breadth of investment team, zero professional turnover," etc., as well as an employee roster. Given the small size of Avalon Capital, little time needed to be spent on committees and the organization chart. In that time, Avalon made the point that they were streamlined for quick implementation and ease of communication between professionals.

The third page dealt with Avalon's valuation disciplines and how they help identify return potential. In Avalon's case, low multiple stocks, dividend growth of ten percent or better over the previous five years, undiscovered assets, and strong management, for example, are sought. This page deals with the reward aspects of the portfolio.

The next page dealt with risk management at Avalon, and was titled "All facets of the organization produce a low level of portfolio risk." The display here was a list of portfolio characteristics vis à vis the S&P 500, demonstrating the low-risk nature of the portfolio. During longer presentations, this and the previous page could be expanded on considerably.

The next page showed a flow chart regarding individual company research, which is meticulous at Avalon Capital. The flow begins with quantitative valuation screens, leading to in-depth fundamental analysis, checks and balances on that analysis, and finally, to the portfolio manager's decision on stock selection, followed by trading and monitoring.

The senior investment professional at Avalon felt more comfortable talking about individual stocks in the portfolio than in philosophical, general terms. Therefore, on the next page, Maria included the ten largest holdings and some specific characteristics of each of those stocks. Depending on the client, and the length of the presentation, the presenter would talk about two or three current stocks in the portfolio and why.

The next page showed factors in the sell decision and how that adds value. Again, since the portfolio manager was more comfortable talking about specifics, Maria decided to illustrate the three sell decisions which were a result of (1) taking profits; (2) minimizing losses; and (3) replacing less-attractive holdings with a better valued stock. Here again, depending upon the length of the presentation, this could be done quickly or extensively commented upon.

The following page focused on the efficient control and review process that assured portfolio consistency. Here, portfolio construction, portfolio review, uniform implementation of the buy/sell decisions, and back-office strengths were detailed in a bullet fashion.

The next page addressed responsive client service in terms of excellent client retention; individualized, timely, and accurate reports; dedicated client service; and a staff prepared to handle increasing assets.

A page describing "How investment results demonstrate success" and highlighting the kinds of markets in which Avalon tends to do best, followed. Also displayed on that page were charts that would illustrate each of the bullets regarding performance relative to the market and other similar managers.

Finally, Avalon and Maria listed the distinctions of Avalon Capital Management and usually customized that page to fit the specific client prospect. For example, if they knew that they might replace a manager because of bad performance, they would emphasize performance characteristics and low-risk style. Avalon's marketing representative is a woman and one of Avalon's partners is Hispanic. They developed a separate, optional page dealing with minority qualifications of Avalon Capital to be used in meetings where they knew that the minority issue would be an advantage.

Avalon attached appendices to the presentation that included biographies of the key professionals, a representative client list, a fee statement, current portfolio holdings, and past twelve months' investments. Again, depending on the prospect, a sample contract, quarterly client report, and ADV could be inserted. During the second year of marketing, Avalon found that using the extensive marketing booklet on initial meetings with staff and consultants prepared the staff well and enabled them to get into more finals. Using a more concise bullet-like presentation in the finals allowed them to specifically address the strengths and weaknesses of Avalon Capital vis à vis the prospect, enabled trustees who were not very knowledgable about Avalon Capital to get a quick view, and ensured that Avalon Capital's presentation would be well within the time limit established by the prospect.

MARKETING STRATEGY—YEAR THREE

Going into Year Three, Avalon Capital was starting to gather momentum. Assets had increased to $180 million in fifteen accounts, and performance was holding up. The overall goals had become less focused on new business marketing and more focused on client service and protecting the investment professional's time spent on structuring the new clients' portfolios. The marketing strategy remained much the same as in Year Two: continue to introduce Avalon to consultants; cultivate existing relationships with consultants and prospective clients; establish a good client servicing schedule to minimize the investment professionals' servicing time; continue to review the marketing materials and one-page fact sheet; and refine and practice the final presentation. Avalon now is considering whether or not to offer a fixed income product to institutions, as the fixed income portion of their balanced portfolios had done quite well over the last four years. In considering that, the decision of whether to hire an in-house marketing staff or continue with the outside representative needs to be addressed.

General Marketing Strategies for Small Firms

The above case study, though fictional, is a very real representation of the phases through which a smaller firm usually passes on the road to becoming a more established, successful firm. The strategy itself is applicable to all asset classes and equity styles; emerging and minority-owned firms. Specifics obviously have to be reworked to match the characteristics of different firms, augmenting the strengths and diminishing the weaknesses. The same thought process and issues are similar for all different kinds of smaller investment managers. The similarities of all of these firms include a small staff with some experience, a short time in business, small assets, and relative obscurity to consultants and the institutional marketplace.

Marketing Minority/Women-Owned Firms

At this writing, a minority- or women-owned investment manager probably has a slight edge in some searches over a similar white-male investment firm. Nevertheless, the professionals have to be above reproach and the product of the highest fiduciary standards of quality and performance. I have never seen a minority-owned firm continue to get business over two or three years without delivering a high-quality, consistent, and superior-performance product.

Successful minority firms have worked very hard for their assets, and have delivered exceptionally competitive results. Poor-performing minority-owned firms have been fired by their clients for quantitative and/or qualitative reasons, such as, professional turnover, inconsistency of style implementation, lack of attentive servicing, and inaccurate reporting/back-office operations. The bottom line is that minority/women qualifications may get you in the door sooner or may give you an opportunity to bid for the institutional business sooner, but you have to deliver.

A women- or minority-owned firm might have an advantage being considered for searches because some institutions, especially public funds, will reduce the qualifications necessary for a minority-owned firm to compete. These are not a reduction of standards of performance excellence, but a reduction in the necessary length of a track record, total assets under management, and length of time the organization has been in business. While there might be an advantage in terms of entry for minority-owned firms, there are distinct disadvantages in terms of the political, social, and emotional tones that are always introduced.

In marketing a minority-owned firm, one has to be very careful to stress the quality of the product and the high fiduciary level of the firm, not to lead with its minority status. That is pretty obvious already. For example, one is likely to encounter pension staff members and trustees who have been passed over by other, less-qualified (in their minds) minorities and/or women for promotion. A major challenge in marketing a minority-owned firm is that the focus can be easily swayed away from the integrity of the investment product to an overall social discussion of what kind of role affirmative action should have in the pension fund. Nearly always, this is not in the best interests of the investment firm.

The challenge is to keep the focus of the meetings and the marketing presentations on the excellence and high quality of the investment product, while more subtly stressing your particular personal credentials and commitment to helping to promote opportunity for minority firms. Overall, it has been my experience that marketing a minority firm has its advantages and disadvantages, but is overall the same as marketing any other newer, smaller, or emerging firm.

The main difference seems to be in the type of questions that prospects ask of a minority-owned firm that, in my experience, were not asked when marketing a majority-owned smaller firm. The questions usually probe the financial safety of the assets—what percentage of the management fee is given to charity or to the community to promote minorities, what insurance does the client have that the principals will not abscond with the assets and concerns that one must "give up" something to hire minorities or women.

The minority investment manager arena, per se, is relatively new, and one would normally expect some strange treatment initially. As minority-owned firms become a greater percentage of the marketplace, and as minority- and women-owned firms demonstrate their capabilities over long periods of time with larger assets, I am convinced that the aspect of marketing minority-owned firms that deals with politics and social issues will decrease. Most experienced, talented, proven minority managers merely want an opportunity to bid for the business, like any other manager, because they know they can uphold the highest standards of fiduciary excellence.

As in any other investment management arena, minority- and women-owned firms will have their share of opportunists and inexperienced managers trying to capitalize on the current and growing interest in promoting and supporting minority-owned firms. Over the long haul, I do not believe those opportunists will be successful, and I firmly believe that the top minority-owned investment firms will rank as high as the top majority-owned firms.

In sum, the *investment* differences in marketing a minority-owned firm as compared with any other smaller, emerging firm are nil. Emotional, social, and political issues that arise in marketing a minority-owned firm are different, and the task is to field those questions and then get the prospects back onto the investment track. How this is addressed within an individual firm is totally dependent on the specific points of view of that firm. In my opinion, a marketer or investment firm that depends on its political and minority status, as opposed to its investment acumen, may get a few token accounts, but will not go the distance to become a strong presence in the industry.

Conclusion

The process for marketing a small, emerging investment-management firm is very much the same as marketing an established larger firm . . . it's just harder, and it takes longer. However, the rewards tend to be greater and more satisfying, as the results can be attributed to several individuals working closely together as a team. If an investment manager continues to focus on doing a great investment job, hires a competent and experienced marketing person, considers the marketer as an equal professionally, trusts his/her judgment and experience and works together, understanding that the marketer's job is just as difficult and important as that of the investment professional, there is a good chance that the assets will grow after a lot of hard work, patience, and tenacity on everyone's part.

An investment firm with reasonably good products and performance that follows a program similar to that outlined in the case study can have a successful marketing effort. It does require teamwork, mutual respect, and a strong commitment, time-wise, financially, and philosophically. To those investment firms who contemplate embarking on a broad-based institutional marketing effort, but who think they can take shortcuts, I offer the following advice: "No marketing is better than bad marketing."

The
Marketing
Process
•
Preparing
to Win

Lessons
in
Financial
Advertising

EDWARD W. GASKIN

We all recognize that the financial services industry is becoming more competitive. Yet the advertising sophistication of institutional financial services has not kept pace.

Why should financial service companies learn how to use this marketing tool more effectively? Let's look at some of the most vital reasons.

Cost-efficiency

Advertising provides an inexpensive way to create awareness of a product. As the marketplace becomes more competitive, advertising is an efficient way to communicate information regarding benefits, combat competitive claims, or register a unique selling proposition in the prospect's mind.

A company may be tempted to stop advertising a product after it has been around a while, but out of sight may very well mean out of mind. "Reminder" advertising will help prevent your prospects from forgetting about your product. Good investment managers are often overlooked at the time of a search, simply because they were "forgotten."

When you make product enhancements, advertising can be used to start the entire process all over again: informing prospects of the development, promoting the benefits of this new enhancement, and registering the selling points.

Companies usually believe that their products are bought for rational investment or economic reasons. This simply is not true. The purchase decision may be rationalized, but we now know that subjective, emotional factors play a very important role in the buying of expensive and complicated products and services. Advertising can create a favorable emotional disposition toward a company or a product.

In business-to-business marketing, there are an average of four buying influences. A sales force is unlikely to know all four. Because the cost of a sales call is approaching $400 by some estimates, it is not effective to cold call in person—advertising paves the way for better sales calls by pre-selling a prospect. Coupon advertising, reply cards, literature offers, etc. can be used to flush previously unknown buyers, or people with an influence on buying, out into the open. Advertising should not be viewed as a necessary evil but as an investment in marketing effectiveness because it can help to shorten the sales cycle. Advertising at adequate frequency can drop the cost of selling twenty to thirty percent.

Competitive Advantage

A company that has not advertised previously has the advantages of starting with a clean slate. This provides a company with the opportunity to describe itself, or its products, in its own terms.

With advertising, a company can completely control when, where, what, how, and to whom its message will be delivered.

A company that advertises, particularly when few of its competitors do, can achieve high top-of-mind awareness. When a prospect thinks about who offers a product, they will automatically think of the company that advertised. A prospect rarely remembers more than five vendors in any product category and once the prospect develops the list, it is very hard to change.

Who Is Responsible?

Financial service companies spend considerable time developing a business plan and the role a particular strategic business unit (SBU) will play in contributing revenues to the company.

But it is one thing to project how much potential profit can be made in a particular area; it is quite another to specify how your company will earn that profit based on a marketing, advertising, and public relations plan for every product in the department.

Often, the manager for a particular department is responsible for advertising the products of the department. The manager of a department in a financial services company probably got the job by knowing finance, not advertising. Consequently, the marketing manager's only concern is that the company "get its name out" so that prospects will have heard of the company before the sales force has to call on them.

This lack of attention becomes a self-fulfilling prophecy: little attention is given to advertising, therefore the advertising is bad and has minimal impact. The manager then feels justified in giving little attention to advertising the next time around.

Three Challenges

There are three challenges in advertising institutional financial services:

- *Creating a relevant difference.* Companies all have similar systems and skilled, dedicated people. The differences are a result of creativity, ingenuity, integrity, and the benefits of different experiences. A company needs to identify and project these differences in a way that is relevant to the marketplace.

- *Communicating value-added services.* Often what makes a product different—or prevents it from being marketed as a commodity—is service. A company needs to communicate these value-added services visually and with copy.

- *Demonstrating benefits in an imaginative way.* The product and its benefits are conceptual and do not easily lend themselves to visual images. Somehow, you need to illustrate or highlight the benefits of the product. The creative people who achieve this produce excellent advertising.

Improving Your Advertising

First, determine your prospects' needs. This sounds easier than it is. Get your hands on as much research about your prospects as you can, and talk with them. The better you know your prospects, the better you can tailor your advertising. Then you can plan your strategy, with the following guidelines in mind.

ADVERTISE PRODUCTS

Part of your strategy must include advertising specific products. Advertising is commonly referred to as "salesmanship in print." The best salesperson can call on no more than eight decision-makers per day. Product ads can be seen as cold calls on thousands of your prospects on a regular basis. The ads can answer important questions prospects have, such as "What can your product do for me?" and "Is your product a complement, alternative, or replacement to the services I currently use?"

Products also move in and out of vogue. Product advertising allows you to advertise your products when they are hot and take advantage of editorial calendars and special sections in print media. This has become increasingly important as the number of financial journals has rapidly multiplied. In addition, products have their own identity. When positioned correctly, brand preference can be created. This has happened in every other industry and there are signs that it is beginning to occur in the institutional financial-services area.

USE A DISTINCTIVE FORMAT

If there is no difference between your product and that of your competitors, create one! If an image is successfully created, then it will be easier for your prospects to remember your product from all the other "me too" products. People still purchase commodities such as Chiquita bananas and Sunkist oranges based on the packaging instead of the product. The choice between two or three major Wall Street institutions for a multi-million-dollar contract may simply come down to "packaging."

One step in doing this is to create a distinctive format for your ads. A prospect should be able to recognize your ad without seeing the logo, signature, or product name. A good example of this is Merrill Lynch's advertisements. One knows a Merrill Lynch ad the moment one sees it. Their format is flexible enough to be used for any of their products from their many different business units. This means that any time any product from the very different business units is advertised, it reinforces the company name. A unified format promotes the company even when the prospect is not interested in the particular product.

NAME YOUR PRODUCT

Naming your product can help in its promotion. There currently is a major difference between consumer products and institutional financial services in this area. The marketers of consumer products spend a great deal of time and money to create the perfect name for a product. Most institutional financial-service products live their entire life with a generic name. In a parity product environment, naming the product provides another opportunity to set yourself apart from your nameless competition.

Some of the best examples come from Salomon Brothers, whose "CARDS" stand for certificates for amortizing revolving debts backed by credit-card receivables; "HOMES," for homeowner-mortgage Eurosecurities; and "CARS," for certificates of automobile receivables. The only thing worse than no name is a bad one. One cash-plus fund is named the C+ fund—surely this is not the best way to convey product quality!

BE INFORMATIVE

Another part of your strategy should include writing more informative ads. Prospects are in the market for a product because they have a specific need. When they are in this fact-finding stage, they want all the information they can get.

Informative ads help to educate most of the people involved in the search process about the strengths of your product. Your prospects' consultants also make it their job to keep up on new products. The results of product advertising are easier to measure than image advertising, because the inquiries from an ad can be recorded.

BE FACTUAL

Prospective buyers for many institutional financial services are controllers, treasurers, financial officers, accountants, and investment professionals who are detail-oriented. They read trade journals for news and information. Informative ads can introduce them to new applications of your product that they probably have not considered. This could help them use your product more efficiently or more extensively.

Although research studies continue to show that longer copy is read more than shorter, some still argue that these busy professionals won't take the time to read it. But no one argues that these same professionals would read a several-page article if they thought it was interesting. If your ad is interesting and informative, your prospects will read it.

BE LIVELY

Your prospect's life is filled with numbers, data, etc. Try to make your ad less cold and impersonal than straight statistical data. One technique is to use humor and illustrations. Cartoon illustrations allow you to dramatize lifeless, intangible benefits that probably could not be shown easily another way. Your prospects will remember a humorous illustration that helps them visualize the benefit longer than one that simply presents the "facts."

Care must be taken when using humor since everyone may not think your ad is funny. Make sure that your prospects are laughing with you instead of at you.

CHOOSE THE RIGHT MEDIA

Media strategy is a very important, but often overlooked, part of the advertising strategy. In advertising, if a tree falls in the forest and no one hears it, the tree did not fall. You can do extensive market research, position the product perfectly, and develop a brilliant series of ads, but if the ads are not in the right place at the right time, all is lost.

When developing a media plan, you must answer the who, what, where, and when questions. Fortunately, a media plan is one of the easiest aspects of advertising to measure, and in yearly reviews, the plan's effectiveness can be analyzed and evaluated.

WHAT TO AVOID

Avoid ads telling the world how great you are: a zillion dollars under management, insured, in capital, issued, placed, sold, bought. You cannot define success on your own terms. The use of objective ratings are better, but only if you tell how it benefits the prospect.

Avoid telling your prospects that you did a million deals in thirty days, yet every customer is special. They will believe that they are just a number, a junior person is working on their account, or that they are not getting a quality product.

Avoid using analogies in an attempt to help prospects visualize benefits. Readers go through print media quickly and often miss the analogy. Sunsets should be kept for travel ads; athletes for sporting ads; animals for zoo ads.

Avoid using images that have nothing to do with your company or its products.

Avoid making your president, team manager, or significant other the star of the ad. Their spouse may be the only one interested. Besides, it detracts from the main point of the ad, which should be how you can help your prospect meet a need.

Avoid making your prospects work to figure out what you are selling, because they won't. They get paid to do something else. The ad should communicate immediately what you are selling so that those who are interested won't miss it. The task is not to entice nonprospects to read the ad, but to make sure that prospects who *are* in the market for your product don't miss the ad.

Finally, get your ads approved by your legal department. There are a myriad of legal issues you must deal with. The last thing you want is for the product and company to receive bad publicity or be sued for not complying with federal regulations.

Conclusion

Investment banking, corporate finance, money management, and other institutional financial services are sold by people very conscious of their appearance. They dress in a way to project a certain image. A company will spend thousands of dollars for travel and entertainment to win a deal that could be worth millions. But the very same company may pay the least attention to the "salesperson" who will communicate with more prospects than all of the company's sales force combined: the company's ads.

There are many benefits of advertising, and a well-executed media plan can provide your company with

competitive advantages. Advertising institutional financial service is not without its difficulties, but the rewards
of good advertising are well worth it.

REFERENCES

"Copy Chaser Criteria," *Business Marketing,* January 1988.

Ogilvy, David, *Ogilvy on Advertising,* First Vintage Books, 1975.

Rapp, Stan, and Collins, *Maxi-Marketing,* McGraw- Hill, 1987.

Roman, Kenneth, and Mado, *How to Advertise,* St. Martin's Press, 1976.

10

Lessons
in
Financial
Public
Relations

EDWARD W. GASKIN

The public relations function in the institutional financial services area is changing. In the past, the goal of public relations was rather simple: project and maintain a good image of the company and its leadership in a local geographic area. Today, the task is more diverse and complex. Companies must establish a quality reputation for a wide range of products in multiple markets.

In the midst of this increased competition, financial companies need every competitive edge they can get. One weapon often overlooked is public relations. Public relations should be an important part of your marketing mix because it can accomplish what other marketing communications cannot. We will discuss reasons why there is a greater need today than ever before for financial services to use public relations—and then describe ways to do so effectively.

Differentiating Quality

The quality of financial services—similar to services provided by other professionals, such as accountants, doctors, and lawyers—is hard to distinguish. Most institutional financial-service products are provided by professionals from reputable companies. The product, price, distribution, and service may be similar. Sometimes the only differences are the intangibles, such as positioning, image, or reputation. Comparing intangibles is subjective, and purchase decisions are often made because one company has done a better job of communicating and maintaining trust and confidence than another.

Even quantitative, objective data can be interpreted differently due to differing perceptions. That is why an investment management firm with the best performance record is not always selected in a money manager search.

A company should use public relations to add value to the basic product, to differentiate the product, and to prevent the product from becoming a commodity.

Maintaining Client Contact

The company/client partnership requires continual communication. Keeping informed about clients' attitudes toward your company, or a particular department or product can prevent the loss of a client by spotting danger signs early. Regular client contact will also provide your company with a steady stream of ideas for new products or product enhancements.

By maintaining regular communication with your clients you can continually "resell" clients by informing them of new hires, product improvements, new services, and how these changes benefit clients. Client contact provides an opportunity to cross sell additional products and/or increase the quantity of a product the client is currently purchasing from you. Public relations can do this through letters, phone calls, newsletters, and client visits, among other, more traditional, public relations activities.

Isolating Bad Publicity

When one part of a company receives bad publicity— such as banks for making bad loans, or brokerage firms for insider trading—the whole company suffers. Bad publicity can cause the prospect to doubt the quality of other services provided by the business, even if there is no connection between the services. By using such techniques as branding and product/department positioning, bad publicity can be contained to the product or department.[1] Crisis management, a particular function of public relations, can limit the financial impact and even turn a bad situation around.

Positioning Multiple Strengths

Although bad publicity may overshadow the entire company, the converse is not true. If a company has a reputation for being a leader in futures and options, few prospects would naturally assume that the company was a leader in cash management or mergers and acquisitions. In fact, a prospect may think that in the era of specialization, if a company is a leader in one field it cannot be a leader in another.

Public relations can help departments and products develop their own separate identity drawing from the strength of the company name, but enabling multiple strengths to be positioned in the prospect's mind.

Establishing a National Presence

Many companies are taking advantage of deregulation to establish a national business. Companies are changing their name so it will be less geographically specific. A company with a very good East Coast reputation may find it is largely distrusted on the West Coast. Most banks established a good reputation in the local community by sponsoring community events. Yet what happens when the whole country becomes your community? Prospects may wonder how committed a national company is to the local area.

Public affairs programs can help relieve these doubts by becoming a good corporate citizen in the community, supporting local nonprofit organizations, and effectively using corporate sponsorships of regional or national interest. Another technique is to generate positive publicity for hiring new employees and vendors and helping the local economy.

Maintaining the Perception of Leadership

It used to be that there were few new products and that the old products did not change often. Today, it seems that in every issue of every financial trade magazine a company is introducing a new product, and competing firms are quick to announce that they have replicated any advances.

Deregulation is moving at a rapid pace, creating a ripple effect on the development of new products. The increase in social activism has had an impact on a variety of financial issues. In addition, the entire financial services area is exploding with growth as more money comes under professional management.

All of this change has left many prospects confused. There is an opportunity for a company to demonstrate leadership by interpreting these events for the marketplace. Also, issues management and lobbying are public relations functions that can be used to maintain industry leadership.

Establishing Credibility in New Markets

When companies enter new markets for the first time, they must establish credibility. It is fairly easy to assume that an insurance company is good at providing insurance. But what will prospects assume when an insurance company becomes a money manager? An even greater problem arises when companies that have little association with the financial services field, such as Xerox Financial Services Corp., enter the market. The name "Xerox" is associated with copiers, not financial services. The prospect may be skeptical about the company's ability to provide a quality product.

As a rule, new products are treated with skepticism because no one knows if the product works, and they don't want to be the first to find out. If the product is coming from an established company, some may buy the product out of faith in the company. A new product from a new company faces an uphill battle for acceptance.

Public relations can help convince prospects that a product is credible and reliable.

Educating Multiple Decision-Makers

Prospects are looking for a product to meet a need. But due to the nature of the purchase they ultimately buy the company. Institutional purchases are decided by one or more committees in a multiple decision process. The level of product knowledge committee members have will vary, but each member will have an opinion about the company. The choice might be between buying a product technically superior from an unknown company and a weaker product from a respected company. The second product may win the sale based on its perceived quality versus its actual quality.

Buyers themselves usually have to justify their decisions to someone else. If a company has a good reputation for quality or is just better known, it will be easier to get the decision through the committee. Public relations can provide materials that educate committee members and increase awareness of a company or a product.

Making Products Memorable

Many companies want to offer a product line as complete as their competitors—competitors who may come from different financial sectors. But that creates a problem for the prospect. For example, which is the most natural to run your company's 401(k) plan: an insurance company, bank, brokerage firm, investment firm, or mutual fund house? The fact that the choice is not obvious illustrates the level of perceived similarity between very different suppliers.

In addition, prospects are becoming less product oriented and more problem/solution oriented. With more products being promoted, prospects can't help but confuse them. The blurring of distinctions and increased clutter makes it more difficult to be seen and remembered.

Usually, a prospect won't remember more than five products or companies per product category. Public relations can use techniques to position your company in prospects' minds as one of the few providers of a service.

Cross-selling of Products

As companies grow, it becomes more difficult for employees to know what businesses their own company encompasses. Often there is considerable opportunity for employees to supply leads to other parts of the company. In addition, the more employees know about the services their company provides, the more resourceful they can become when trying to package a product or solve a client's problem. Not only does this help maintain high levels of customer service, it helps the company stay innovative.

The institutional financial services area is profitable and growing, but there will be continued shakeouts, and the best products won't necessarily make it. The products that survive will come from companies that have effectively positioned themselves. Public relations is an effective tool that can help accomplish these critical goals.

Steps to Effective Public Relations

First, it is necessary to reconceptualize what public relations is and what it can do. It is more than answering a reporter's inquiry or sending out periodic news releases. Public relations is often thought of as "free publicity," but is far from free. It takes commitment from your company in terms of time and money.

Second, you must have a position statement. Your position statement should reflect the company's mission and culture in terms of your clients. This will provide direction for how the company desires to be portrayed in the media. You cannot, however, position yourself as something you are not. Through research you can also measure the difference between how you wish to be perceived and how you actually are viewed by clients and prospects.

Third, you should have gathered enough current information to develop a situational analysis. What is occurring in the surrounding environment? Are there any new competitors, products, or markets? Are there any new laws or technological developments that could have an impact on your company or product? Who are the key opinion leaders and groups you should keep in touch with? This list will no doubt include community, business and political leaders, media people, and your employees, clients, investors, and prospects. It is necessary to develop a communications system that will receive as well as distribute information. This two-way process is part of your company's market intelligence network.

Fourth, you must develop a pro-active plan. This means prioritizing what is to be promoted, then seeking out opportunities

- writing booklets, articles, news releases, and position papers;

- launching new products;

- developing exhibits for trade shows and conventions;

- speaking at trade or industry conferences; and

- staging/sponsoring events.

Fifth, you need to determine how you will respond to media inquiries. This "responding plan" will require several steps, such as

- developing an expert source list, press kits, product literature, and position papers;

- monitoring emerging issues;

- determining what products or events might make your company vulnerable, such as legal/ethical issues, market volatility, bad loans, client relationships, or product failure; and

- thinking through a procedure to handle crisis public relations situations.

Sixth, develop a budget that will help you implement your plan and accomplish your objectives. You should get maximum marketing mileage from a piece once it is developed. For example, after a speech is given at a conference, a copy might be sent to a reporter who may develop a story on that topic. You may also turn the speech into an article for publication. Reprints can then be made and sent to clients and prospects.

Seventh, manage and coordinate your activities. Once the public relations plan is complete, it will not implement itself; someone must manage the process. Someone must assign responsibilities and be accountable for the plan's success or failure. In addition, the plan should be coordinated as much as possible with advertising and sales management activities to get the most efficient use of resources and effort.

Eighth, measure your results. How many mentions, bylines, or features did you receive? How many qualified leads did your newsletter, trade show exhibit, or article produce?

Ninth, evaluate and start the planning process for the next year. What worked, what didn't, and why? Were your objectives reached? How can things be done better? List the ways the company as a whole and marketing in particular benefited from the public relations program.

Tenth, remember public relations works best when it produces a direct or implied third-party endorsement. Examples of direct support are word-of-mouth references, testimonials, case studies, and publicity. Implied endorsements may include such things as having an article published, being selected to speak at a conference, or being quoted in the press. These types of endorsements are very useful tools in the hands of skillful salespeople—and making the sale is what it is all about.

REFERENCES

Bivins, T., *Handbook for Public Relations Writing,* NTC Business Books, Lincolnwood, IL, 1988.

Cutlip, S. M., Center, A. H., Broom, G. M., *Effective Public Relations 6th Edition,* Prentice Hall Inc., Englewood Cliffs, NJ, 1985.

Goldman, J., *Public Relations in the Marketing Mix,* NTC Business Books, Lincolnwood, IL, 1984.

Hart, N.A., editor, *Effective Corporate Relations,* McGraw-Hill Book Company, London, 1987.

NOTES

[1] For example, Tylenol received bad publicity when people were poisoned . This resulted in people not buying Tylenol for a while, but they did not stop buying Johnson & Johnson products.

Evaluating Simulations— Caveat Emptor

HUGH M. NEUBURGER

Private Consultant

Amidst the welter of investment information that plan sponsors need to analyze, nothing is more difficult than evaluating simulations. Yet pension plans stand to gain a lot from identifying winning investment strategies and avoiding losing ones. In an effort to assist plan sponsors and marketers creating simulations, here are some guidelines for reviewing simulations of investment products.

Simulations are not the same, and it is crucial to distinguish among them.

To avoid ambiguity, let's clarify the meaning of the word *simulate*. Paraphrasing *Webster's Ninth New Collegiate Dictionary*, one finds two meanings for *simulate*: (1) "to make an imitative representation of the functioning of one system or process by means of the functioning of another"; or (2) "to assume the outward qualities or appearance of, often with the intent to deceive." In investment management, simulations are commonly used to provide a hypothetical performance record for a product or approach that has no actual performance record. If this hypothetical record has arisen from doubtful methods or calculations, then deception can occur in the sense that a faulty product or approach may assume the appearance of a viable one. Armed with the right questions, plan sponsors can separate the good ideas from the bad and avoid being deceived.

Simulations are not all the same. There are three types of simulations, and it is worth the effort to probe a bit in order to distinguish among them. One type is the *ex post* simulation, meaning a simulation done after the fact using all available, pertinent information. A second type is the *ex post* simulation in which some available information is not used. In this case, an effort is made to do the simulation as if it were before the fact, but it is actually done after the fact. The third type is the *ex ante* simulation, meaning before the fact. The way to distinguish among the three types of simulations is to ask two simple questions: (1) what information was *known* at the time the simulation was done? and (2) what information was *used* in performing the simulation?

Ex post Simulations

In the first type of *ex post* simulation, an investment manager has and uses financial market and economic data for the period of the simulation. An *ex post* simulation of this kind tells us what investment result would have been obtained if a manager *had known* the data needed to make some investment decisions. Hindsight confers a tremendous advantage on people who already know what everyone else has had to forecast. This advantage usually translates into very attractive simulated investment returns. Take as an example, valuing equities with a dividend discount model. Being able to use actual past discount rates and dividend growth rates rather than estimates is sure to improve the results a manager obtains.

In the second type of *ex post* simulation, in which some pertinent and available information is excluded, the advantage of hindsight is lessened, although not eliminated entirely. A manager can develop an investment approach using data from 1975 to 1985 and then *"pretend"* to know neither financial market nor economic data for the years 1985 through 1988. The data from period 1985 to 1988 are called a "hold-out sample" because these data are "held out" or not used in developing the investment approach. Simulations using data from a hold-out sample are intended to show what investment results would have been obtained if a manager *had*

not known the data needed to make some investment decisions. In this case, decisions have to have been
based on a manager's estimates or forecasts. Caution is
needed in evaluating "pretended" ignorance. Even
with the best of intentions, a manager may find it hard
to ignore information that was widely disseminated
and analyzed before some research was done. For example, if one knows that bond investors were heavily
influenced by money supply growth during some past
period, that knowledge will help a manager. Even without using the exact data, the manager, often without
realizing it, knows how investors acted and uses that
knowledge.

Let us take a moment to review how these *ex post*
simulations are actually done. Suppose that I were to
offer a simulation showing my ability to predict the
monthly return to the U.S. bond market as measured by
the Shearson Government Corporate Composite Index.
My approach to bond management is to predict the inflation rate and the change in the Treasury bill rate one
month ahead. How does my strategy work? My simulation will show that if at the end of December I know the
January inflation and Treasury bill rates, then I can use
this information to predict the January bond return and
act accordingly. The following equation is my simulation
for the period 1973 through 1985.

The t-test statistics given in parentheses under the
coefficients of Equation 1 indicate that the inflation rate
and the change in the Treasury bill rate do explain the
bond return. The adjusted coefficient of determination
(R^2) shows that about twenty-one percent of the bond
return is explained. Other statistics show that this regres-
sion equation has been properly estimated. When looked
at only on a statistical basis, the simulation seems to be

EQUATION 1

$$(SHGCC)_t = \begin{array}{c} 1.40 \\ (3.80) \end{array} - \begin{array}{c} 1.10\,(DTBL)_t \\ (-5.89) \end{array} - \begin{array}{c} 1.11\,(CPI)_t \\ (-1.90) \end{array}$$

$$\bar{R}^2 = 0.212 \qquad DW = 2.13$$

where:
SHGCC = monthly return of the Shearson Government Coporate Composite Index
DTBL = monthly change in the rate on three-month U.S. Treasury bills
CPI = monthly growth rate of the consumer price index

sound. What makes the simulation a doubtful basis for an investment strategy is that the required inflation and bill rate data were only available *ex post*. I did not have the crucial data before the start of each month, when these data would have been needed to use my strategy.

We can easily carry this example a step further by treating the years 1986 through 1988 as a hold-out sample. I will claim that my one-month-ahead predictions of the inflation rate and the change in the bill rate have been used for this three-year period. By combining data from 1973 through 1985 with data from the hold-out sample, an equation can be estimated for the period 1973 through 1988. This simulation is Equation 2.

EQUATION 2

$$(SHGCC)_t = \begin{array}{c} 1.27 \\ (4.48) \end{array} - \begin{array}{c} 1.10\,(DTBL)_t \\ (-6.19) \end{array} - \begin{array}{c} 1.00\,(CPI)_t \\ (-2.06) \end{array}$$

$$\bar{R}^2 = 0.195 \qquad DW = 2.14$$

The results obtained in Equation 2 are substantially the same as those obtained in Equation 1. Does the hold-out sample make Equation 2 a credible simulation? Perhaps, but not necessarily. The answer depends upon the methods used to produce the one-month-ahead predictions of the inflation and bill rates. Were these predictions produced with data that were not available before the inflation and bill rates themselves? Before accepting as meaningful a simulation like Equation 2, one needs to determine whether any data used in the hold-out period were available only *ex post.* Often use of a hold-out sample merely disguises an *ex post* bias that would otherwise have been obvious.

Ex ante Simulations

In an *ex ante* simulation, the manager must use estimates or forecasts to drive an investment process because the actual economic and financial data are not available at the time the investment decisions that depend upon them must be made. This kind of simulation tells us what investment results would have been obtained if the manager *could not have known* essential data when investment decisions were made. Because we know this manager had to rely on forecasts or estimates of essential data, we can interpret an *ex ante* simulation as a test of the manager's ability to forecast; this ability is an essential part of any active investment style. Of course, forecasts have to be dated to prove knowledge before the fact. Often a manager with a substantial record of forecasts or estimates will prefer to show an actual performance record, but a simulation based on legitimate forecasts can be a sound way of showing the potential value of those forecasts. The *ex ante* character of the simulation is preserved as long as the forecasts were made without knowledge of latter events and were

EXHIBIT 1 Forecasts of the Real S&P 500 Return

Forecast Release Date	Period of Forecast	Forecast Return	Actual Return
June 26, 1987	7/87	-1.52%	4.78%
July 29, 1987	8/87	3.79%	3.18%
August 28, 1987	9/87	-1.55%	-2.70%
September 29, 1987	10/87	-5.22%	-21.67%
October 28, 1987	11/87	-2.32%	-8.31%
November 27, 1987	12/87	2.09%	7.59%

available before the simulated investment decisions had to be made.

An example of an *ex ante* simulation can be given without providing the statistical details given in illustrating *ex post* simulations. Suffice it to say that much more sophisticated statistical methods have been used to produce the following forecasts of the real S&P 500 return (Exhibit I).

The forecast release dates show that these forecasts were available in time for an investor to act upon them before the time periods covered by the forecasts had begun. Following some reasonable strategy, an investor will certainly do well with such forecasts if they are accurate. Of course, investors may also want to know how forecasts are produced, but release dates are enough to establish the *ex ante* character of the approach.

There are a number of flaws that invalidate simulations. Hindsight is the most common and serious of these. A simulator's knowledge of a past period should not be confused with predictive ability. The bias arising from hindsight is obvious in the case of an *ex post* simulation. Even when a hold-out sample is used, hindsight can play a role. Specific data can be held out, but the general character of a product or approach may reflect knowledge of a period that would not have been available before the fact. Using the example of bond investors' concern about the money supply, a manager may know this concern was stronger in some periods and weaker in others and structure the simulation accordingly.

Simulators' bad assumptions can also undermine simulations. Some of the most flagrant examples of simulators' bad assumptions involve their treatment of transaction costs. For this reason, special scrutiny is required to distinguish simulators' fantasies from market reality. Some simulations merely show the performance of buy lists with no adjustment for transaction costs at all. Zero transaction costs is a very bad assumption. Realism requires a sensible allowance for commissions and a decrement for market impact based on the liquidity of the names traded and the timing of trading. While there is room for disagreement about the magnitude of transaction costs in developed markets like those for stocks and bonds, there is not much room for argument about the characteristics of markets before they existed. For instance, to assume there was a market for S&P 500 futures contracts before 1981 is an extremely doubtful basis for a simulation. Traders must deal with real brokers and real market conditions; no trader has the luxury of assuming a market that does not exist.

Another flaw to be aware of is a change in market conditions. Assumptions about market conditions, either hidden or explicit, may be built into an investment approach. For example, there have been extended periods when growth, value, or smaller capitalization stocks have been in favor. Conditions which prevail during a simulation period and are assumed to validate a simulation may change once an approach is used real-time. At the very least, it is necessary to identify the assumptions upon which an approach is based. Then some judgement can be made about how likely those conditions are to persist.

Treating simulations as tools to enhance our understanding gives us a helpful perspective. Like other tools, simulations may be used well or poorly. The only way to judge a simulation is to know what question it is able to answer and then to consider whether the answer is what one wants to know. If we want to know whether a product or approach is viable, we need a true *ex ante* simulation. If properly done using *bona fide,* dated forecasts, this kind of simulation shows forecasting power and the ability to use good forecasts. Those who are skeptical about all simulations can take comfort from the fact that *ex ante* simulations are very resistant to distortion.

In the case of *ex post* simulations, the rule to be guided by is *caveat emptor.* Remember the biases that pervade simulations of this kind. Even the most scrupulous investment managers find it difficult to avoid using all the information they have regardless of any claims to the contrary. Focusing on the questions I have outlined can help create a simulation which will pass the test.

How to
Shorten
the
Sell Cycle

DANA DAKIN

President,
Dakin & Willison

The institutional investment field is known for the long lead time often required to close a sale. However, it is possible to shorten the sell cycle and, simultaneously, improve the quality of the overall sales effort.

Many barriers confront investment marketers today: the "big ticket" commitment required, the fiduciary responsibilities, and the increasing sophistication and competitiveness of the field. In order to break down these barriers and accelerate the sell cycle, it is useful to divide the sales process into four distinct phases, each requiring a different approach.

Phase One: Position Your Product

The barriers you must overcome at the beginning of the sales process are either the prospect's total ignorance of the product, or the second-hand impressions picked up via the grapevine or the media. In either case, your first step is to articulate a strong, credible case for exactly what it is you have to offer.

This means you must develop a well-written, thorough, and logical "proof statement" of precisely how your product works and what makes it different. The statement should not be built around the numbers you've achieved—too many people are still trying to make past performance the central focus of their sales effort—but rather, it should detail the key points of your investment philosophy and what value that philosophy can be expected to add in the future. Only when this context is created does past performance become truly meaningful.

Many firms essentially skip this critical step. They do so for a number of reasons:

- Fully describing an investment philosophy takes work;

- Portfolio managers fear being pinned down;

- It is assumed that "the numbers speak for themselves"; and

- The architects of the product often want to divorce themselves from the sales process.

It is true that this phase could be safely bypassed in the early, relatively unsophisticated days of this business. But it's dangerous now: the institutional knowledge base has grown tremendously over the years and the information you provide must meet higher standards.

In committing the resources needed to produce a truly credible and sophisticated product story, a story that moves beyond what we call "plagiarized boilerplate," you will create an extremely powerful platform from which to launch a more efficient and effective sales effort.

Phase Two: Predispose the Gatekeeper

With a strong positioning statement in hand, the next challenge is to get the attention of the gatekeepers and bring them up to speed on your product. The objective at this phase is to get them "predisposed" toward you so that they can, in turn, sell the ultimate decision-makers on giving you a hearing.

The role of the salesperson at this stage is primarily educational. You need to take the time to capture the gatekeeper's imagination with the logic of your concept, supporting it with ample evidence, including your positioning package. This will provide real momentum to the sales process by making the gatekeepers so comfortable with your product that they can speak with real conviction.

A cautionary note: it is vital that this educational effort include a genuine two-way information exchange. Your well-thought-out positioning piece will provide an effective and impressive "primer" on your product. However, beyond this, it is also extremely important for the salesperson to elicit from the gatekeepers a complete understanding of the prospects' specific needs as well as what they consider to be the strengths and weaknesses of your product vis-à-vis those needs.

With this invaluable input, it is then possible to craft a well-targeted, client-driven presentation for "the committee."

Phase Three: Persuading the Committee

In presenting to the pension committee, it is important not to assume that you can simply repeat verbatim the presentation that sold the gatekeeper.

As we all know, few things are as fast-changing, or as complex, as the investment business. Prior to meeting with committee members, it is vital to confirm with the gatekeepers what the prospects' current concerns are, as well as their sophistication level, and adjust your presentation accordingly.

When you're in front of the committee, believability is the name of the game. You're now speaking directly with the people who carry the risk for choosing your firm and, given the traditional "beauty contest" approach with its lineup of short presentations, you must establish credibility in a highly compressed time frame.

The most effective way to do this is to focus on using your past results to demonstrate the tightness of your investment process. If you link your performance directly to the process—as well as explain how your portfolio managers drive the process—you will significantly reduce the probability of being eliminated.

In addition, leave no important questions unanswered: questions not addressed give grounds for elimination. Again, the committee is trying to confirm that your investment process is essentially foolproof. If an issue constantly comes up in the Q & A, you need to rebuild your presentation.

Finally, don't go on "automatic" when you're in front of the committee. People do business with people. The committee members must not only like your logic; they must also get a strong sense of who you are and what you stand for, all in a very short period of time.

Be rehearsed. Be articulate. But also be yourself. It will win you more finals than any "canned" sales pitch.

Phase Four: Perpetuating the Sale

The sell cycle does not end when the contract is signed. In many ways, it just begins. The need to constantly reaffirm the viability of your investment process is crucial to continuing the relationship and adding cash flow.

A well-thought-out client retention program is as much a part of the sales process as the initial selling effort. It goes beyond the old ritual of perfunctory client meetings, a bit of scrambling at each quarter's end to get the numbers out, and "touch-base" phone calls when something goes wrong.

An effective client retention effort combines education and full disclosure utilizing timely, face-to-face meetings; regular, informative phone calls; and quarterly letters and annual reviews that explain exactly how results were achieved. If you use every possible opportunity to reestablish client comfort and resell your investment process, you will earn the trust and respect necessary to perpetuate the sale.

13

Making the Most of the Marketing Budget

STEPHEN J. DARBY, JR.

*Executive Vice President,
United States Trust Company
of New York*

One of the joys of anthologies is their diversity of opinion and insight. And the brevity of the assorted parts. While this may relieve potential boredom, it often lacks a context.

So let's back up a little and attempt to put this subject in perspective. It is also a convenient device for confessing to my prejudices about budgets and the process.

Budgets seldom are what they should, or could, be. In good times they are ignored, but in bad times they are confining. They can assume a sanctified station far beyond their functional importance. In the absence of well-devised and mutually shared policies and strategies, the budget fills the void. Instead of sensible financial guideposts to business development, "the numbers" dominate when imagination and foresight are missing or weak. Once devised, reviewed, re-reviewed, and adopted, budgets ossify. Flexibility is sacrificed for the etched-in-stone character of the budget. Guideline becomes commandment.

How unfortunate. How unnecessary. Moses gave us all the stone tablets we need, a long time ago.

To understand the extent of the influence of the budget process in your organization, consider the amount of time and effort spent on the preparation, discussion, revision, formal presentation, and adoption of the overall budget and its marketing component. Contrast that with the attention to developing, evaluating, and modifying the business plan and the marketing plan. Examine the spirit of the exercise. Is the process making policy?

The Foundation

Before a realistic marketing budget can be developed, there must be a comprehensive marketing plan conceived and adopted. Before adoption can be expected, an evaluation of the firm's marketing status—a marketing audit—should have been conducted, assessing candidly the strengths and weaknesses, opportunities and limitations, and corrective measures required to improve the firm's competitive position.

In short, the budget is the final stage, a financial expression of the investment management firm or division's business philosophy, business plan, and marketing strategy. The budget's scope and composition reflect them.

What do we want and realistically expect to accomplish in our marketing program? What resources do we require? What priorities do we establish in the allocation of those resources to the most advantageous market opportunities for us? What financial commitment is needed to prepare for the future?

Resources aren't endless. Money usually will be more tight than abundant. Choices will be hard and judgement critical. Wishes will give way to reality. But the decisions will be made in the context of the business plan designed for the firm. Everyone in the organization should then be working from a commonly shared frame of reference.

Constructing a Marketing Budget

Having said that a marketing budget is an extension and financial expression of a business and marketing plan, it is obvious that marketing budgets will be different among firms. All the variables that differentiate firms, their products, sales organizations, and circumstances will influence their budgets, to say nothing of the attitude of senior management and the orientation of the firm itself to the essential necessity of client acquisition and retention.

Single-product/service firms will adopt different approaches from multiservice firms. Generalist and product-specialized sales staffs will require different strategies and budget choices. Market-oriented, generalist sales staffs should benefit from market-specific budgets, perhaps to supplement more universal marketing programs.

Rather than constructing a model budget or describing a specific example with little relevance to your particular situation, I prefer, instead, to discuss some of the things to consider in selecting components of a marketing budget. The inclusion of any, and their relative proportions, in your budget will be determined by your judgement of their appropriateness to your marketing plan.

Components of the Marketing Budget

For the purpose of this discussion, the sales function has been set apart from the other components of the marketing process. This editorial preference should not diminish the primary importance of a professional, well-managed sales effort. Without it, the marketing expenditures are largely wasteful.

The marketing budget items that we'll examine will be those that support the sales organization: advertising, public relations, sales literature, directed promotions and mail campaigns, conferences and seminars, general mailings and communications, marketing information systems, market research, and product development.

ADVERTISING

No single budget component will generate more heated debate. Everyone has an opinion of the efficacy of advertising. Most of them are negative. Face it—it's an uphill battle, especially difficult in harder financial times.

Print advertising is the only choice for most of us, television being reserved for only the deepest-pocketed. The trade press in our field is limited, requiring that ads be original and distinctive to gain attention. Grudgingly allocated, limited dollars do not attract serious agency attention, putting the burden of creation often on the inexperienced.

To put your advertising expectations and allocations in perspective, return to the focus of your marketing plan. If you need to make the firm more visible and gain name recognition, select those publications which demonstrably reach your widest, targeted audience, or concentrate on specific groups of potential clients. Cite product/service skills or chosen specialties. Select editions that will feature articles or information of interest to your targeted prospects or are related to your specialties. If possible, be repetitive in your ad placements.

And be prepared to follow up with active prospect contact. The ads will create awareness. Repetition will prompt recall. They will sell nothing. People do that, in this business.

In the earliest stages of start-up, renewal, or new product/service introduction, the primary benefit of print advertising—name awareness—is vital. Well-known firms seldom face the financial necessity of abandoning meaningful advertising programs. Faced with less financial freedom, once a firm is sufficiently satisfied that name recognition has been established, budget allocations should increase for audience-specific promotions and programs.

DIRECTED PROMOTIONS AND PROGRAMS

Simply stated, these are marketing projects that are targeted to specific prospects, where the attendee or recipient is clearly identified by name and affiliation. The obvious examples are sponsored seminars or conferences and special mail campaigns.

Sponsored meetings offer logistical and administrative convenience, audience selection influence, and limited, noncompeting cosponsorship, often abetted by valuable market research. Though the agendas are academic and generic, the forums serve to showcase a firm's professional capabilities and talents preparatory to further contact.

Sponsored seminars and conferences are one of the most cost-effective marketing expenditures. Ideally, they should be selected to highlight specific investment skills, especially new services, and to reach those market segments less readily accessible, such as the endowment and foundation market.

Special mail promotions come in a variety of forms. Certain financial publications, for example, offer programs that provide a chosen audience with complimentary subscriptions or reference volumes from one or more sponsoring investment management firms. Such programs are an effective alternative to print advertising in the attempt to achieve or reinforce name recognition among a targeted group of plan sponsors.

A note of caution. Don't expect that directed, prospect-specific promotions or programs will deliver anything but a cost, unless a well-devised and timely program of followup is enacted.

PUBLIC RELATIONS

Everyone is happy with "third-party" references. They look relatively inexpensive, almost free. But the process is often misunderstood and, to many, threatening when encountered.

Good media and public relations are no accident. They are the product of well-conceived and executed programs, most often relying upon externally provided professional assistance. That costs money, and should be carefully monitored to assure a high level of skilled attention.

Unless you can piggyback the shared cost of a parent company-sponsored public relations program, or find a capable, independent consultant in the field, try to make the most of senior officer visibility and involvement in the industry. Their membership in associations and consultant- or publication-sponsored institutes, personal speaking engagements, availability to the press, and authorship of articles in professional and business journals are to be encouraged. As someone responsible for the marketing program, you should help to develop opportunities for recognition of the investment professionals and actively participate in any and all of such activities, if you can. This is time and, of course, money, too. But, it's off budget.

Another word of caution here. Many people are uncomfortable in speaking situations, particularly to large audiences. They are unfamiliar with television broadcasting. They have a fear of being misquoted by the press.

Don't budget or attempt anything of this type, if you have concerns. Consider presentation skill training and media relations coaching instead.

GENERAL MAILINGS AND COMMUNICATIONS

A beginning caveat. In this business, we are accused of the deforestation of America. Blanket mailings and the mailing of unwanted communications are wasteful and unproductive. Don't mail what can't be followed up promptly—if you must mail.

Where prospect contact includes informational mailings, send only what they want, when they want it. Separate information into discrete subject, data categories, or modules. If performance is of interest, have it separate from the economic and market outlooks, or vice versa. Less is more. And you've more of your marketing budget to put to better use.

MARKETING MATERIALS

I tend to think of this principally as sales literature. For standard product information, go further with the modular concept, and break your products and services into separate, succinct one-page presentations. (OK—front and back are acceptable.) Spend your budget dollars on perfecting and staffing desktop publishing capacity. Your product/service messages can be concisely and attractively presented. There is no economy in using a comprehensive brochure, especially one that is expensively produced, for a multiproduct firm. No one is going to buy everything you're selling, especially at one time. More effort at prequalification, and more attention to listening, should enable more precise presentations.

For the obligatory corporate brochure, avoid the costly tendency to portray picture and pedigree of virtually everyone on the professional staff. Use a companion "contact" sheet of photos and abbreviated bios, if you must. Reprinting is costly and turnover is a fact of life.

For those with a creative bent, and some budgetary latitude, the new world of communication sophistication is opening up rapidly. Who would have predicted the widespread use of VCRs? Or CDs—and in the car, no less? Think about it.

MARKETING INFORMATION SYSTEMS

If you have more than one salesperson, offer more than a single product or service, or value your sanity and that of your colleagues, set about investigating and installing a compatible sales and marketing information system. More than just a facility for sales-tracking and prospect followup, these systems provide communication ease and management reporting simplicity. They are indispensable to any organized sales effort and are readily available without expensive development cost.

MARKET RESEARCH

To cut down the escalating cost of travel, cold calling, and the waste of blind mail campaigns, seek out sources of market research that indicate prospective interest in new products, managerial changes, and asset redistributions. Firms with established clientele would be well served to build into their budgets an evaluation of client satisfaction.

RESEARCH AND DEVELOPMENT

The most underattended area in this business. It is one thing to know which of your services may be of interest to prospective clients. It is equally, perhaps more, important to devote attention to identifying emerging client needs. "Consumer research," new product development, and market testing must be included in budgets.

In an increasingly crowded and maturing marketplace, the future will belong to firms that anticipate and respond creatively to changing client requirements. The most significant growth in assets will be achieved by those firms that address real client needs by not merely offering what's on the shelf.

To Conclude, a Look Ahead

Sorry. No easy solutions. No simplified budget allocation among categories of possible or necessary expenditure. No line-item simplicity. The final mixture, the prescription for relief within your organization, lies in your diagnosis of the problem. And, as with any diagnosis, a comparison is necessary with normally desirable behavior.

The business and marketing plans form the basis of intelligent comparison. They are the true test of the necessity of budget allocations and expenditures. Endorsed by senior management, commonly accepted throughout the organization, their guiding principles prevent the "tyranny of the budget" from stifling growth.

Marketing and marketing management hold the keys to future success. Credible and consistent investment returns are the expected end product of the manufacturing process. Marketing imagination will determine whose products will be more readily accepted in the market-place. Creatively conceived marketing plans will give rise to marketing budgets that are judged by their purpose, not their size. They will be less vulnerable to simplistic cost containment and cost reduction measures because their importance will be better understood.

And so we enter a new era. Modern Portfolio Theory gives way to Modern Marketing Theory.

The
Finals
•
Winning
the
Account

Selecting
the
Finalists

DAVID A. DAVENPORT

Assistant Treasurer,
Lord Corporation

I'm sure that if Vince Lombardi had been an investment manager, he would have said: "Performance isn't everything. It's the only thing." The pension manager's fiduciary responsibility is to hire the Vince Lombardis of investment managers—the managers who will provide winning results, year after year. The challenge is to find the Vince Lombardi managers, to analyze the candidates' win/loss record to find the consistent winners.

After many of the necessary functions required for an effective search have been performed—developing the questionnaire, sorting managers by the fund's parameters, and visiting the top contenders—you must now subject the remaining managers' performance record to an intensive analysis. This analysis should be completely objective and quantitative. While you may have determined your favorites as a result of your visits and conversations, you must test the performance results of all of the finalist managers on an equal footing. Marketers interested in analyzing their chances can also benefit by this process.

Determining how to objectively analyze performance results is a difficult task. After looking at performance from many different angles, I have found that an objective approach can be developed in a fairly logical and straightforward manner. First, to satisfy the statisticians, we should include as many observations as possible in the analysis in order to derive meaningful conclusions. Using the manager's quarterly returns for a long time period, ten years' minimum if possible, will be sufficient. Second, we should measure the percentage of quarters that are better than the fund's equity benchmark, the average amount that these observations exceed the benchmark, and the volatility of those observations.

It is interesting that few, if any, money managers state

the frequency with which they beat their benchmark. I have never seen a money manager claim that they consistently beat the S&P 500 "X" percent of the time. That is too revealing a statistic. But it is exactly why we are hiring them—to beat the benchmark in a majority of cases.

Rather than stating an annualized return, why not reveal the average number of basis points that the manager has been able to beat the market per quarter? It does not matter if the market is up or down since our long-term asset allocation strategy is structured to provide the expected long-range returns. We are hiring active managers to beat the market, period. A quarterly increase/decrease type of measurement basis eliminates the arbitrary selection of the most favorable time periods for a manager to state annualized returns.

By determining the number of quarters in the manager's record, the percentage of quarters that the manager outperformed, and the average basis points of incremental performance, the sponsor has established a much better standard for a true comparison of performance. In addition, the performance evaluation can then be taken one crucial step further by adjusting the returns for risk. By measuring the standard deviation of these incremental returns, a simple spreadsheet calculation, the sponsor can determine the level of risk taken to generate these returns and can calculate a risk-adjusted return. The sponsor then has a fair and objective method for comparing and ranking investment manager candidates. All of these concepts will be developed and illustrated in this article.

For simplicity, it is assumed that your fund's equity benchmark is the most common one, the Standard & Poor's 500. The S&P 500 is the benchmark for most money managers. Since the S&P index contains five hundred issues, it is broad enough to capture most of the movement of the U.S. equity market. If the sponsor is selecting a manager style that is not appropriate to the S&P 500 benchmark, such as a small capitalization manager, he would use another benchmark, such as the Russell 2000 or the NASDAQ composite.

It is preferable to analyze your managers' results in both good and bad markets and over several market cycles. However, over the past ten years, the market has been primarily in an upward trend. Most of today's managers have been in business less than ten years, which makes such measurements not possible. It is said that two-thirds of today's money managers have never experienced a sustained bear market. They have enjoyed only an unprecedented bull market. The average manager today may not be prepared to weather a severe bear market storm. In such cases, you have no choice but to satisfy yourself that your managers have a battle plan for bear market investing and the disciplines and fortitude to protect the plan's portfolio during a protracted down market cycle.

Standard Deviation

There are two dimensions to investment performance, risk and return. In order to analyze the returns of the investment managers, one must understand the risk that is taken to generate those returns. Standard deviation is a common statistical measurement of risk.

The definition of standard deviation is unenlightening: standard deviation is a statistical measure of the variation or dispersion of a sample from the mean of a sample.

However, by breaking up standard deviation into a series of small steps, it becomes easily understandable.

Let's take a series of numbers and determine the standard deviation:

4, 8, 8, 4

While a true standard deviation calculation should be based on a much larger series of numbers, using this small series will aid in understanding the concept.

We first calculate the arithmetic mean—the traditional average—of the series, which is six. The standard deviation is simply the variation of the numbers in the series from the average of the series.

We can already see that the variation for the numbers in this series from the average is two units: each number varies from the average (six) by two. This average difference from the mean is known as the mean absolute deviation. While this is an easy measure of dispersion to understand and interpret, it is rather unsuitable for an accurate mathematical analysis of combined series of numbers. A few more steps need to be taken.

To determine a mathematically accurate measurement of dispersion, you first must calculate the variance of all the numbers. To determine the variance, you first determine the differences for each number in the series compared with the average and then calculate the square of the differences.

As shown in Table I, the difference is squared to provide absolute numbers (eliminate negative numbers). The variance is the sum of the squared differences (sixteen) divided by the number of observations (four), which calculates to a variance of four units. The standard deviation is the square root of the variance, in this case two units.

The standard deviation measures the extent of the variation of returns from the mean that we may expect.

TABLE I

(Average) –	(Number) =	(Difference)	(Difference)^2
6	4	2	4
6	8	–2	4
6	8	–2	4
6	4	2	4

A table of probabilities shows that approximately two-thirds of the data (more precisely 68.27 percent) lie within plus or minus one standard deviation for a normal distribution.

Therefore, in the above series, the results, two-thirds of the time, will deviate plus or minus two from the average between four and eight. If more confidence is required, two standard deviations are used to reach a ninety-five percent probability. In the above example, two standard deviations (two times our standard deviation of two) is four. Nintey-five percent of the time, the numbers will vary by four from the average—between two and ten.

To summarize, the numbers below show the average of the series and the expected range that the numbers in the series will vary sixty-eight percent of the time (one standard deviation) and, for a higher probability, ninety-five percent of the time (two standard deviations).

Average	One Standard Deviation	Two Standard Deviations
6	4 to 8	2 to 10

In investment analysis, our concern for standard deviation is linked to our desire to understand the variability or distribution of returns that we can expect over time. In a normal distribution, data can be plotted on a smooth, continuous, symmetrical bell-shaped curve with a single peak in the center of distribution. The bell-shaped curve for the above series of numbers is depicted in Figure I. A straight line segments the curve into one and two standard deviations.

For the sake of clarity, Table II shows more series of numbers, listed from low to high standard deviation, with the mean, the variance, and the standard deviation.

As each number in the series varies from the mean by greater amounts, the standard deviation increases. Note that the relationship between the numbers in each series is exactly the same: the high number in the series is exactly double that of the low number in the series.

Note that even though the relationship of the individual numbers is exactly the same, the standard deviation increases as the absolute numbers increase. This increase in the standard deviation for each series is cru-

FIGURE I Standard Deviation of Returns

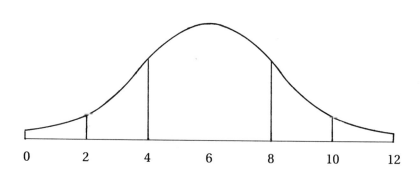

TABLE II

Series	1	2	4	8	16	32
	2	4	8	16	32	64
	2	4	8	16	32	64
	1	2	4	8	16	32
Mean	1.50	3	6	12	24	48
Variance	.25	1	4	16	64	256
Standard Deviation	.50	1	2	4	8	16

cial, since it confirms the mathematical validity of the calculation for its application in equity investing and investment manager returns. For example, you would be little concerned if the return on one dollar invested varied by fifty percent but would be very concerned with the same volatility for a $1,000 investment.

As the total value of investments in the pension plan increases, there is greater concern that the volatility of returns does not increase. As the plan grows, diversification should increase as investments are spread out over a wider variety of issues. Increasing diversification serves to dampen the volatility of the quarter-to-quarter returns.

Performance Analysis

By now you have determined the time period you will analyze (typically ten years or more) and have requested quarterly results over this period from your finalist managers. As an example of the series of analytical steps to be taken, quarterly results will be used from the eleven-year period of 1977 to 1987. While this was mostly an uptrending market, the market did suffer declines in 1977 (down 7.2 percent) and 1981 (down 4.9 percent). The fourth-quarter 1987 was a significant down quarter—the S&P 500 declined 22.5 percent—but the total year equity return was up 5.3 percent.

You will need to gather the quarterly results of the benchmark, easily available from several sources, such as your master trustee, a performance evaluation service, or the public library. Set up the spreadsheet as depicted in Table III.

The Lotus DAVG function is a database statistical function that will determine the percentage of quarters that are above and below the benchmark. In order to return the proper values, it is important that the spreadsheet be set up exactly as shown, especially Rows 7 through 11.

First enter the S&P quarterly results, starting in Row 11, Column D. The first manager's results, Manager A, are entered starting in Row 11, Column G. Manager B's results are entered in Row 11, Column J and so on. Managers A and B are the two highest-ranked value managers. Managers C and D are the two highest-ranked growth managers.

Note in this example that manager B did not start managing funds until mid-1977, and the first investment returns were achieved in the fourth quarter 1977. Therefore, the cells for the first three quarters are left blank. It is necessary to leave the spreadsheet cells completely blank for the time periods when the managers were not actively managing money so that the cells are not part of the spreadsheet calculations of the manager's mean returns.

The columns following the quarterly results are the increases or decreases of the managers' quarterly returns compared with the benchmark. These returns are excess S&P 500 returns, unannualized percentage points. For

TABLE III   Quarterly Performance Analysis

	A	B	CD	E	FG	H	I	J	K	L	M	N	O	P	QR
1															
2				MANAGER SEARCH PERFORMANCE ANALYSIS											
3															
4		BENCHMARK			MANAGER'S QUARTERLY PERFORMANCE										
5		S&P500			COMPARED TO BENCHMARK (+/-)										
6		BENCHMARK			+/-	+/-		+/-	+/-		+/-	+/-		+/-	+/-
7		VARIABLES			0.0	1.0		0.0	1.0		0.0	1.0		0.0	1.0
8															
9	YEAR	QTR	S&P	+/-	MGR A	+/-		MGR B	+/-		MGR C	+/-		MGR D	+/-
10															
11	1977	1	-7.5	0.0	-1.7	5.8					-5.3	2.2		-6.2	1.3
12		2	3.3	0.0	11.1	7.8					2.2	-1.1		5.2	1.9
13		3	-2.8	0.0	-2.4	0.4					-3.5	-0.7		-3.8	-1.0
14		4	-0.1	0.0	5.6	5.7		12.6	12.7		0.3	0.4		5.0	5.1
15	1978	1	-5.0	0.0	4.6	9.6		10.3	15.3		-1.7	3.3		2.2	7.2
16		2	8.4	0.0	12.7	4.3		11.3	2.9		6.7	-1.7		12.0	3.6
17		3	8.7	0.0	14.4	5.7		3.0	-5.7		7.8	-0.9		18.7	10.0
18		4	-5.0	0.0	-9.7	-4.7		-4.5	0.5		-7.0	-2.0		-17.1	-12.1
19	1979	1	7.1	0.0	13.6	6.5		6.5	-0.6		13.1	6.0		2.3	-4.8

example, the formula for Row 11, Column H is +D11–G11 (the S&P return of –7.5 percent less Manager A's return of –1.7 percent). In this example, Manager A outperformed the S&P by 5.8 percentage points, since he suffered that much less of a decline. The formula for Manager C in Row 11, Column N is +D11–M11, and so on. Copy this formula down the total number of columns for which there are quarterly results.

For the benchmark increase/decrease column, place zeros in Column E. We will be using this column as a baseline when graphs are generated. We will graph the managers' returns as an increase or decrease from the benchmark baseline of zero. A point above the baseline is outperformance, a point below is underperformance.

We want to see as many points as possible over the bench-mark baseline.

Summary of Quarterly Results

The summary of the managers' quarterly results will appear as depicted in Table IV.

There are six main measurement categories that are discussed in detail below.

CATEGORY 1: PERCENT QUARTERS UP

In Category 1, percent quarters up is the percentage of quarters in which the manager's returns were above that of the S&P 500. Manager A's performance results cover eleven years, or forty-four quarters. In thirty-one of those forty-four quarters (70.5 percent of the time), their results were better than the S&P 500. This is clearly superior performance. While this manager is an excellent candidate, this category is only one part of the total performance measurement analysis. We still need to determine the risk factors and other relative return data.

CATEGORY 2: PERCENT QUARTERS DOWN

Category 2 contains the percentage of quarters in which the manager's returns were below that of the bench-mark. It is exactly the opposite of percent quarters up. While seemingly not necessary to calculate this percentage, it is a check number that serves to verify the accuracy of the previous calculation. If the two numbers, both calculated independently, do not add up to one-hundred percent, there is an error in the spreadsheet.

TABLE IV   Summary of Quarterly Results

QUARTERLY RETURNS RELATIVE TO BENCHMARK	MGR A	MGR B	MGR C	MGR D
1 % QTRS UP	70.5%	63.4%	61.4%	63.6%
2 % QTRS DOWN	29.5%	36.6%	38.6%	36.4%
3 MEAN INC/DEC	2.08	2.30	1.77	1.85
4 AVG WINNING QTR	3.85	5.32	3.99	4.67
5 AVG LOSING QTR	(2.15)	(2.95)	(1.76)	(3.08)
6 STD DEVIATION	3.76	5.27	3.56	5.04
RISK ADJ SCORE (1*3)/6) (HIGHEST = BEST)	0.389	0.277	0.304	0.234

EXPECTED RANGE OF RETURNS	MGR A	MGR B	MGR C	MGR D
+ 2 STD. DEV.	9.61	12.83	8.90	11.94
+ 1 STD. DEV.	5.84	7.56	5.33	6.89
MEAN	2.08	2.30	1.77	1.85
- 1 STD. DEV.	(1.69)	(2.97)	(1.80)	(3.19)
- 2 STD. DEV.	(5.45)	(8.24)	(5.36)	(8.23)
ACTUAL BEST QTR.	10.00	15.30	9.50	14.70
ACTUAL WORST QTR.	(4.90)	(5.70)	(6.30)	(12.10)

CATEGORY 3: MEAN

Category 3, the mean, is the average of all increases and decreases for each manager relative to the benchmark. For our purposes, the mean is the expected return of the manager relative to the benchmark. In the case of Manager A, he has outperformed the benchmark by 2.08 percentage points for all quarters. This is an additive number to the benchmark quarterly return. For example, if the benchmark is up an absolute 3.00 percent for a quarter, Manager A will, on average, be up 5.08 percent. If it is down 3.00 percent, the manager will be down only .92 percent.

CATEGORY 4: AVERAGE WINNING QUARTER

Category 4 is the average quarterly increase when the manager performs better than the benchmark. Manager A has an average winning quarter increase of 3.85. When Manager A's performance is better than the benchmark (in thirty-one of forty-four quarters), it is above the benchmark by 3.85 percentage points. When he is good, he is very good.

CATEGORY 5: AVERAGE LOSING QUARTER

Category 5 is the average quarterly decrease when the manager's performance is less than that of the benchmark. Therefore, when Manager A's performance is under the benchmark (thirteen of forty-four quarters), it is down an average of 2.15 percentage points. When his performance is bad, it's not too bad. There is some downside protection when this manager is underperforming the benchmark.

CATEGORY 6: STANDARD DEVIATION

The standard deviation, category number 6, is the standard deviation of the increase/decrease columns. We are comparing the standard deviation to the increase/decrease of returns relative to the benchmark rather than the standard deviation of the returns themselves. We are concerned more with how the returns deviate from the benchmark than the deviation of the returns themselves. This is a bit of a twist on how managers would calculate their own standard deviation.

The reason is that plan sponsors should be more concerned with how the manager performs against the benchmark than the absolute returns. Our long-term asset allocation study has verified an appropriate percentage allocation of funds to the equity sector. This specific allocation will provide most of the long-term returns for the pension plan. The plan executive's responsibility is to select the managers that will perform well in relationship to the fund's benchmark.

A measurement of standard deviation of the relative returns provides a more realistic and tighter measurement of the volatility of a manager's returns. Remember that standard deviation calculated by this method cannot be compared with standard deviation calculated elsewhere. Our calculation is specific to the search and is calculated using a distinct range of variances to the benchmark. It cannot be compared with standard deviation of returns as calculated by the manager.

Expected Range of Returns

The expected range of returns section in Table IV depicts the dispersion of returns around the manager's mean return. The mean return is shown between the most likely range of returns (plus or minus one standard deviation) and the best/worst range of returns (plus or minus two standard deviations). The highs and lows of performance can easily be compared.

Besides comparing an average return, the sponsor has a basis for comparing the expected ranges of return. In addition, the actual best and worst quarter for each manager is depicted to highlight any extreme variances from the expected range that the sponsor may want to explore. For example, consider the two extreme best and worst returns for Manager D. The sponsor should question the manager about the strategy and diversification in place that caused this type of unexpected volatility.

Performance Conclusions

There are three crucial expectations for an investment manager's performance:

- You want a manager who will on average outperform the benchmark on a quarter-by-quarter basis.

- Since your manager's returns are measured and reported quarterly, you want a manager whose returns are better than the benchmark's a majority of the time.

- Your manager must not take undue risks to achieve this performance. Volatility, measured as the standard deviation of quarterly returns, must therefore be reasonable.

Comparing returns with a benchmark is not only valid but preferred for the consistency analysis we are performing. To measure consistency, we prefer a manager who outperforms the benchmark in a clear majority of cases but not necessarily by large margins. A manager who consistently outperforms the benchmark by only a small amount, after fees and transactions costs, will, over time, outperform the manager who has excellent but very volatile performance.

When Manager A's performance is better than the benchmark, it is better by 3.85 percentage points. When his performance is less than the benchmark, his performance is worse by 2.15 percentage points. On the whole his performance is better 70.5 percent of the time, and he outperforms by 2.08 percentage points on average. Compared with the other managers his standard deviation is not excessive.

Now compare Manager B to Manager A. Manager B has a higher average quarterly increase of 2.30 percent versus 2.08 percent. All other things being equal, you would select Manager B since he has the highest quarterly returns. However, all things are not equal. Manager B is taking higher risks to obtain those results as evidenced by a much higher standard deviation (a standard deviation of 5.27 percent versus 3.76 percent for Manager A).

Notice how the average quarterly increases and average quarterly decreases between the two managers differ markedly. Manager B is up quite a bit more in the increase column (up 5.32 percent versus 3.85 percent for Manager A) and is also down more in the decrease column (down 2.95 versus 2.15). Manager B is outperforming the benchmark 63 percent of the time while manager A is up almost 71 percent of the time.

If you have to choose one manager, which do you choose? One manager has slightly better returns and significantly higher standard deviation. Interesting dilemmas arise when we are forced to consider the dark side of performance—risk. Consider Figure II, which depicts the range of quarterly returns for our four managers. This graph shows the mean quarterly performance above the S&P 500 for the eleven years and the range plus or minus two standard deviations.

Consider the returns of Manager A and Manager B, as illustrated in Table V. Manager B's mean return is ten percent higher than Manager A. Since his volatility is also higher, his range of returns, plus or minus two standard deviations, is greater than Manager A on both the upside

FIGURE II   Range of Quarterly Returns Relative to S&P 500
Plus or Minus 2 Standard Deviations

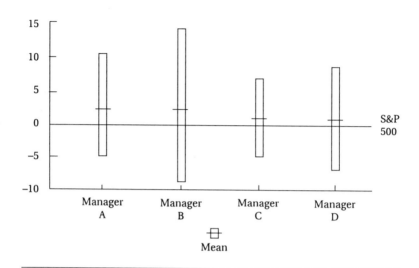

TABLE V   Comparison of Managers' Returns

Standard Deviation	Manager A	Manager B	%
% Quarterly Returns:			
+ Two Standard Deviations	9.60	12.84	25%
+ One Standard Deviation	5.84	7.57	23%
Mean	2.08	2.30	10%
- Two Standard Deviations	(1.68)	(2.97)	43%
- One Standard Deviation	(5.44)	(8.24)	34%

and the downside. His return on the upside, two standard deviations, is 12.84 percentage points, which is
twenty-five percent greater than Manager A, but also

thirty-four percent greater on the downside for two standard deviations.

Should a plan sponsor accept a ten percent greater return for twenty-nine percent greater standard deviation?

Risk-Adjusted Return: The Coefficient of Variation

A method to resolve the risk/reward dilemma is the coefficient of variation, which is solved by dividing the mean expectation (R) by the standard deviation (σ):

$$V = \frac{R}{\sigma}$$

This measures performance adjusted for the level of market risk taken to achieve this performance. It is a method for comparing performance in two dimensions, risk and reward. Managers should not be ranked on reward alone, and the coefficient of variation calculation draws the risk factor into view.

Taking this concept one step further, we can develop an enhanced risk-adjusted score (S) by first multiplying the mean (X) times the percentage quarters up (%U), and then dividing this result by standard deviation (σ).

$$S = \frac{X\,(\%U)}{\sigma}$$

The "percentage quarters up" is used in the formula to give an edge to the managers who have a higher percentage of quarters that outperform the index. This serves to increase the consistency of positive returns relative to the benchmark for the pension fund. The objective is to hire the best performing managers in terms of superior returns, reasonable risk, and the number of times the index is outperformed. The enhanced risk-adjusted score factors for that objective.

The higher the score the better. You will notice that this works remarkably well when you compare the risk-adjusted scores with the other performance results of the managers that are illustrated in the example. Manager A is clearly preferred to Manager B.

In these examples, Manager A scores much higher on a risk-adjusted basis that Manager B. In short, his results, while slightly lower on average, were more consistent. In this example drawn from real life, Manager A's results are the result of a very disciplined buy-and-sell strategy that is rigorously followed. There have been no changes in the strategy since inception of the firm. The client portfolios are well diversified and the firm was fully invested at all times.

Manager B also has excellent results but they are more the result of a "star" stock-picker of the firm—the founder who devotes a huge amount of time and resources to select and sell stocks. The firm was not always fully invested as it developed new themes to invest in. This was an excellent firm that used plenty of raw intelligence and hard work to get results.

As a result of the questionnaire, the visit, and the analysis of quarterly results, the sponsor should feel very comfortable in ranking Manager A over Manager B, or, of course, hiring both managers. The sponsor clearly understands the performance and investment strategies of both managers, a perception that would not have been obtained if he had hired a consultant to do the search for him.

Risk Histogram

Since we are looking at each quarter's returns and how they deviate from the benchmark, another revealing method of depicting a manager's returns is a histogram of the distribution of returns relative to a benchmark.

Figure III illustrates the number of quarters that Manager A's returns were above or below the S&P 500. For example, Manager A's returns were from zero to plus two percentage points above the S&P 500 returns a total of eleven times for the forty-four quarters in our search period. Note the bulk of the distribution is in the plus S&P range of the histogram.

**FIGURE III Distribution of Returns for Manager A—
Relative to S&P 500**

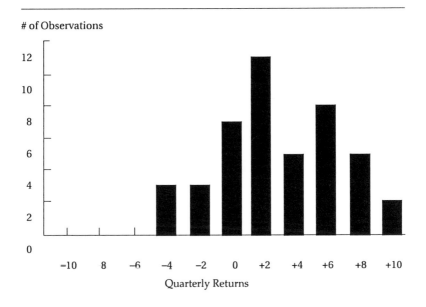

# of Observations

Quarterly Returns

**FIGURE IV Distribution of Returns for Average Manager—
Relative to S&P 500**

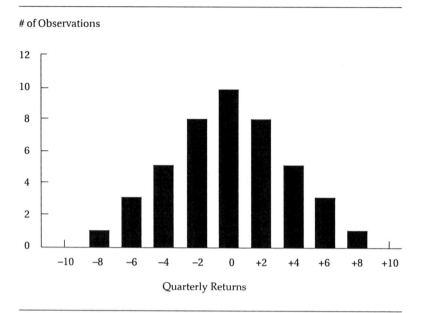

# of Observations

Quarterly Returns

This is in contrast to a manager whom we will call the "average manager," who has returns equal to the S&P but with the same standard deviation as Manager A. This hypothetical manager's distribution is shown in Figure IV. These returns are equally distributed around the zero return amount, the center of the graph.

This histogram is a rather simple but effective way of illustrating how an above-average manager deviates in a positive manner from the norm of market returns. Try asking one of your investment managers to show his returns this way!

Risk Adverse Investors

A central theme in classic risk analysis in the early 1950s was based on Dr. Harry Markowitz's studies.[1] Dr. Markowitz, referred to as the father of modern portfolio theory, pointed out that the goal of modern portfolio theory is not solely to maximize the expected rate of return. He noted that the investor considers expected return a desirable thing and variance of return an undesirable thing.

He contended that investors are risk adverse, that they expect a certain rate of return with minimum standard deviation. For example, an investor would prefer an investment with a higher expected return of ten percent and a standard deviation of two percent over an investment with an equal expected return of ten percent but a standard deviation of four percent.

Investors would rather have their returns dispersed closely around an expected return than experience wider swings in returns for a similar expected return. Therefore, most investors try to minimize the deviations from the expected return by diversifying. They construct a portfolio with a number of dissimilar securities and the securities of companies in different industries.

While diversification serves to ensure market-like returns, today's investment manager faces increasing pressure to improve his return performance. Performance is becoming increasingly difficult due to several factors, namely, the huge size of assets under management, the growing sophistication of competing money managers, and the heartbreaking challenge of the modern market itself.

One way to increase returns and lure pension plan money is to take increasing risk. Unless the plan sponsor understands this temptation and can adjust performance for risk, there is the danger of hiring too much risk for too many dollars. The risk-adjusted score that we have calculated for our finalist managers is an attempt to measure how well the individual investment manager has diversified his portfolio and how much risk is being taken to achieve a desired expected return.

Selecting One Manager

Once you have entered the quarterly results for all the managers into the spreadsheet and calculated the scores, you can rank all the managers. If you are selecting just one manager, you should be able to select your winner easily. You need not rely exclusively on the risk-adjusted score, but you should have a good rationale for deviating from it. If the total scores are reasonably close among several managers, you should use the experience gained from the visits to pick the manager you are most comfortable with.

Now that you have intensely analyzed the individual manager returns, you will find that you have a better common ground to discuss returns with your candidate managers in a more informed manner. No longer can they discuss performance the way they would prefer and which has been closely developed in their marketing material.

They must now discuss both return and risk. They must illustrate more clearly how their investment strategy does or does not provide consistency of return along with reasonable risk. You the sponsor, much to their chagrin, can demonstrate how well they have actually performed over a large number of observations in a manner that is relatively free of distortion. Not only will you gain their respect, but as you question them about their periods of outperformance and underperformance, you will truly understand how they perform, when they perform, and how much risk is involved. It is a much more rewarding discussion. For managers, being prepared for such questions will make the meeting a more rewarding experience.

If you have decided to select several managers, which I highly recommend if you have sufficient funds to allocate, you should experiment with various combinations of managers to determine which composite will produce the best results. By combining the returns of several managers as a team, you will increase diversification and lower risk to the point where the consolidated returns of the team will be nearly as high and the standard deviation lower or almost as low as that of any of the individual team members.

NOTES

[1] Markowitz, Harry M., "Portfolio Selection," *Journal of Finance*, vol. 7, no. 1., pp. 77–91.

Some Thoughts on Selecting an Equity Investment Manager

L. DUNCAN SMITH

*Senior Vice President,
Frank Russell Company*

A decision to invest assets in something other than United States Treasury bills reflects a willingness to accept the risk inherent in other asset classes. To identify the successful risk-takers among active managers, we must first understand the nature of the risks associated with a particular organization's investment approach. We must then assess the resources at the organization's command and how they are used in an effort to accept risk wisely.

Three Active Management Techniques

An investment organization given an index as a benchmark is limited to using three techniques in an effort to provide superior relative results:

1. Disinvestment—The manager can elect to place a portion of the portfolio's assets in types of securities that are not included in the index—cash being the most obvious one.

2. Structure skewing—The manager can analyze the index and then intentionally build portfolios that are structured differently. The most common applications involve broad economic sector or industry diversification. However, a manager may also emphasize low P/E, high yield, low price-to-book, etc. as an initial screen to identify the universe from which portfolios will be constructed. That this is a strategic decision at the structural level is not always understood by the manager; however, such *a priori* structural decisions will have a dominant influence on interim portfolio results.

3. Asset selection—This is the decision as to which security to purchase or sell.

Sales presentations frequently give lip service to all three elements. However, experience has shown that an organization usually places a greater emphasis on one of them or that the decisions made in one of the areas will exert the dominant influence on downstream results.

Thinking in Terms of Equity Manager Styles

It is often useful to remember that the equation defining the return on an equity investment is relatively simple:

$$\text{ROR} = \text{dividend yield} + \text{change in earnings} + \text{or} - \text{change in P/E}$$

The equation is also useful in explaining our three broad U.S. equity styles.

As "price" is included in both yield and P/E, it is obvious that price-driven managers will tend to focus on these elements of the equation. In the case of the contrarian manager, the focus is almost entirely on pure price, usually a depressed one that, in the manager's view, represents an over-discount of whatever problems the company is currently experiencing.

Earnings growth managers, on the other hand, will tend to put more emphasis on the middle variable of the equation —change in earnings. These organizations will devote considerable effort to forecasting future earnings streams and will pay relatively little attention, if any, to assessing the degree to which the current P/E ratio may already reflect an adequate discount of at least the next year or two of expected earnings growth.

The market-oriented managers have a more balanced view of the equity market but still tend to reflect some bias toward either the earnings or price element of the investment equation.

Important Components of the Investment Process

RESPONSIBILITY FOR INVESTMENT DECISIONS

Once the investor has identified the principal area of risk accepted by the manager, it is useful to try to identify the individual or group responsible for determining how much of that type of risk should be taken. Again, I have biases—this time toward clear accountability, which is another way of saying that I do not like committees or group-think approaches to arriving at investment policy or strategy decisions. Where a group is involved, it is usually necessary to try to determine whether it functions "democratically" or merely serves as a forum for airing different views before someone (perhaps the chief investment officer) decides what stance the organization will adopt. The "democratic" process tends to militate against the unconventional thinker and will ultimately lead to a high degree of uniformity across portfolios. This, in due course, will almost certainly result in average performance, which is likely to be viewed as mediocre relative to a passive benchmark.

RELATIVE IMPORTANCE OF PORTFOLIO MANAGEMENT AND RESEARCH

It is also extremely important to determine whether the organization is portfolio manager-driven or research-driven. If portfolios are highly uniform across the shop, the odds are that the process is research-driven. This indicates that considerable attention should be given to the source of ideas and the quality of the people responsible for making the buy and sell decisions from the research side. Whenever an organization operates with a very large "approved list" (one hundred or more names), it is unlikely that portfolios will have a high level of similarity, and the portfolio manager has obviously become a critical link to the ultimate investment results. It is then important to identify the number of issues held in a typical portfolio. For example, if a portfolio has thirty-five to forty names and the approved list has 150, there is considerable latitude afforded the portfolio manager.

Another point: We tend to prefer organizations that combine the portfolio management and analyst function. While I feel strongly that this improves the quality of judgements made at the portfolio level, we must recognize that it can also dilute the analytical effort during periods of rapid account acquisitions or periods of poor relative performance when client "hand-holding" must be increased. This can result in a vicious circle.

Some organizations follow the practice of promoting successful analysts to be portfolio managers. This may reflect a more lucrative career path for portfolio management than for research and is not necessarily a good sign. Furthermore, someone's success as an analyst does not guarantee equal success as a portfolio manager. In fact, the successful analyst may be unsuccessful as a portfolio manager because of an unwillingness to act decisively on information provided by others.

STOCK WEIGHTINGS

Another area of appropriate focus is how stocks are weighted in the portfolio. I find it particularly insightful to examine the portion of the portfolio represented by the ten largest holdings. If the portfolio has sixty issues, suggesting an average weighting of 1.7 percent, but the ten largest holdings represent forty-five percent, it indicates that the portfolio manager tends to make meaningful bets on some stocks. If this is done at the time of entry (the buy point), what gives the portfolio manager the degree of confidence suggested by the two to three times average weighting accorded the ten most heavily weighted issues? On the other hand, the heavy-weighted issues are often older holdings that have simply outgrown the portfolio and have thus become more significant factors in determining future return. If the ten largest holdings read like household names, this may very well be the case.

BUY/SELL DECISIONS

Another area to test during the interview process is the degree to which portfolios are kept "fresh." In other words, what are the implications for portfolios if an issue is placed on the buy list or given a source of funds rating by an analyst? If portfolio managers are required to sell issues so rated in favor of the buy-list candidates, the portfolios will have a fresher tone than if they may exercise full discretion over such decisions.

We place considerable emphasis on trying to identify a manager's sell disciplines. I believe this reflects the conventional wisdom that having sell disciplines is an important aspect of the investment process. Personally, I feel that we are chasing our tail. The decision to sell a stock is often driven by specific events (price drop or runup) or the need to generate funds to purchase another issue considered more attractive. The best portfolio managers, however, have an innate ability to assess issues (both those owned and potential candidates) in the context of the aggregate portfolio. For these individuals, it is impossible to quantify a precise sell discipline. Thus, I tend to get a bit suspicious when an organization has highly structured sell disciplines, as these suggest a dilution of the portfolio management thought process in favor of mechanical rules.

One sell discipline I find particularly unattractive is "when fundamentals deteriorate." When this happens, you can rest assured that the price of the stock has already declined significantly. Thus, this "discipline" does little to protect assets. Equally unattractive is the automatic sale of an issue when it reaches the price target originally established at the time of purchase. Assuming that the issue may have been held for six to eighteen months, it has always seemed to me that the original price target should be reevaluated in light of new information that has become available during the holding period.

USE OF CASH

One of my personal shibboleths is a manager that claims to raise cash only as a residual of the issue selection process. An organization which describes market timing in these terms is unwilling to be categorized as a manager that places a lot of emphasis on the disinvestment tactic as a way of beating the index. I argue that with at least ninety-five percent of the organizations claiming that cash is the residual of the selection process, a *sub rosa* market judgement is involved. With the exception of organizations that use absolute screens, some subset of the market will always meet their particular criteria. When they are "unable to find acceptable investments," what they are really saying is that they don't like what their screening techniques are currently producing given the current market environment.

ORGANIZATIONAL STABILITY

One final impression worth kicking around a bit is the stability of the organization's people. Certainly, the key professionals should have been in place across the period of the performance record we are examining. However, an absence of turnover may also indicate an environment in which underperformers are tolerated. Further, I believe the analysts within a firm can benefit from turnover, as replacing them will bring fresh views into the shop.

Portfolio Managers in Presentations

JACQUELINE L. CHARNLEY

Chairman of the Board

CHRISTINE M. RØSTVOLD

President,
Charnley & Røstvold, Inc.

Charisma, leadership, credibility, sensitivity—all contribute to the power of portfolio managers in presentations and impact the results of the presentation. Portfolio managers play exceedingly important roles in a variety of presentations, including:

- initial presentations to introduce prospects to the investment decision-making process and the investment team;

- presentations to manager search consultants to gain endorsement;

- internal research and management presentations to determine investment strategy and holdings;

- final new business presentations to close the sale; and

- client meetings/presentations to retain clients, increase cash flow, and cross-sell a firm's other investment products.

In today's fiercely competitive environment, it is insufficient for portfolio managers to be solely great investors; they must have or develop strong communication skills as well. In all of the above cases, the potential for gaining business is strong, but the outcome rests on the portfolio managers' abilities to

- be a team player;

- communicate clearly, concisely, and honestly;

- establish rapport and credibility;

- listen and respond;

- convey positive enthusiasm;

- convince, persuade, and inspire;

- educate; and

- sell and resell.

Initial Prospect Presentations

Depending on an investment management firm's target market(s), one to several meetings, culminating in a formal presentation before a committee, can be required to win new business. In most firms, sales professionals initiate relationships with prospects and qualify areas of interest. In others, portfolio managers conduct their own marketing. Both approaches have advantages.

When sales professionals conduct the prospecting, the portfolio manager's time is conserved for prospects qualified as having serious interest in the investment firm. With the highly competitive nature of the market, however, and the fact that plan sponsors are inundated with calls and mail from prospective managers, salespeople are finding it increasingly difficult to attain meetings with prospective clients. Salespeople who can bring a portfolio manager to a prospect presentation, or portfolio managers who call directly, generally have the highest success rate in getting meetings.

In addition, many sponsors insist on meeting the portfolio manager prior to recommending a firm to their committees. The value of the portfolio manager participating in prospect presentations is his/her level of familiarity with portfolio holdings and the investment decision-making process. The portfolio manager can cover the investment process, discuss portfolio characteristics, show that the firm does what they say they do, and overcome any objections.

The first priority of a prospect presentation is to get another meeting. Time is limited; therefore, the manager must focus on

- identifying the prospect's needs and possible concerns;

- communicating concisely the investment firm's competitive strengths and distinctions; and

- creating an interest on behalf of the prospect to learn more about the investment firm's process and how the style benefits the prospect's investment program.

Key to the success of most presentations is sensitive listening; however, in prospecting, listening is absolutely the most valuable competitive tool a manager has. In these meetings, the portfolio manager can identify how best to meet the prospect's needs. In addition to the factual information the prospect may provide, his/her questions and objections can indicate interests, sensitivities, and concerns. The portfolio manager can also ask questions of the prospect concerning investment objectives, satisfaction with the current program, future proposed changes, and time frame.

After the meeting, if both a salesperson and portfolio manager attend, a debriefing session will ensure that all the prospect's needs and concerns are identified accurately. A pro-active followup strategy can be defined. Generally, a salesperson oversees followup to prospect meetings. When a portfolio manager, however, takes the initiative to respond to a specific issue or concern of the prospect, it is clear that the portfolio manager wants the business. Responding with personalized followup shows that the manager listened, helping to increase the likelihood of getting a second meeting or invitation to a final presentation.

Manager Search Consultant Presentations

Manager search consultants are a strong force in institutional investments and are growing in influence in the private wealth area. Consultants can be friend or foe, and the investment firm that works well with manager search consultants has a definite advantage. As with prospects, the portfolio manager has a major impact on the success of these relationships.

Most consultants do not recommend an investment firm until they have met the key decision-makers and often the entire investment team. The consultant needs to be comfortable with

- the investment philosophy;

- the logic and rationale behind the process;

- adherence to the investment style;

- the strengths, commitment, and contributions of the firm's professionals; and

- performance.

To maximize success with search consultants, managers should understand the consultant firm's business and procedures. What type of consulting services does the firm offer, and who are their clients? Who is responsible for manager research? How is a manager search program conducted? What information (and in what format and frequency) does the consultant like to receive?

Most search consultants have demanding workloads and are deluged with calls and meetings with investment firms. To ensure that time with the consultant is most productive, the portfolio manager should call for an appointment only when he/she has valuable information to share (e.g., new products to introduce or significant changes to the firm or investment process). Calls should not be made just to provide performance updates, and any time constraints set by the consultant should be honored.

Whenever possible, the portfolio manager should encourage a dialogue versus a monologue or boilerplate presentation. The consultant, however, should be allowed to orchestrate all sessions. Either a formal presentation or informal question/answer session will generally be requested. During meetings, focus should be on the investment approach and distinctions, any concerns raised by the consultant, and the strengths of the team. The manager should also be prepared to respond to questions concerning the investment firm's growth objectives and business plan.

Any criticisms concerning competitors should be avoided. Often the negative information is inaccurate. Acting on hearsay undermines the manager's credibility and can lead to the consultant recommending the competitor.

Search consultants will only recommend a manager if they learn what they need to know. Frequently, managers use the majority of their time with consultants asking questions about the consultant's firm, and too little time communicating reasons the investment firm should be included in the consultant's universe. It is best for portfolio managers to reserve their questions until the end of the meeting.

Once a manager starts working with a search consultant, it is essential that the manager respond to consultant requests graciously and promptly. Most managers complain about the time required for consultant questionnaires, unreasonable deadlines, or the lack of qualified analysts. The few managers who do not denigrate consultants stand out.

Portfolio managers can also build credibility by keeping the consultant current on all changes at the investment firm. Consultants, like plan sponsors, do not like surprises. If a consultant's client hears upsetting news about one of their managers before the consultant (who is paid to monitor the managers), the consultant looks bad. A copy of correspondence to any client in common with the consultant is advisable. Even if an investment firm has problems that may prompt the consultant to consider recommending termination, it is best for the manager to inform the consultant of the problem as soon as possible. Never hide negative news from a consultant during a presentation or meeting with a mutual client.

The portfolio manager can further enhance consultant relationships by helping to educate the consultant. Giving the consultant copies of any studies the manager conducts or information on industry trends, new specialty investment strategies, and issues impacting pension funds will be greatly appreciated.

Internal Research and Management Presentations

Portfolio managers frequently must sell their investment ideas internally to other portfolio managers and analysts. The key ingredients for success are quite similar to those required to sell a prospective client: thorough data gathering; convincing presentation of the idea; and the ability to answer questions effectively and overcome objections.

Even after an idea becomes a holding, the portfolio manager must continue to resell the reasons for holding the security and defend the position against other equally compelling opportunities.

Final New Business Presentations

Once the opportunity for a sale is created, a formal presentation before the prospect's committee is usually scheduled. In some instances, it may be a rubber stamp meeting. In other cases, this meeting is critical to whether the prospect becomes a client and the outcome rests on the portfolio manager. Some managers may even walk into the presentation as the favored choice, then blow the presentation and eliminate themselves.

Preparation increases success. The portfolio manager must know as much as possible about the prospect's company and industry. The manager should be clear about the prospect's agenda, issues of primary importance, preferred format, likely questions and objections, and time constraints.

One reason a very successful investment firm has achieved a near-perfect closing ratio is the team's commitment to rehearsal. Prior to final presentations, the presenters spend one-half to one full day rehearsing the presentation and responses to anticipated questions and/ or objections. The presenters, led by the salesperson, decide who will cover certain sections of the presentation and who will respond to which questions. Plan sponsors have commented that the presentation is "thorough" and "obviously well prepared."

Team presentations with the salesperson who initiated the relationship and the portfolio manager who will manage the account are more successful in closing business than solo and/or monologue presentations. To maximize the benefits of team presenting, informal exchange and supportive interjections between presenters throughout the presentation are effective. When an associate is presenting, the portfolio manager must pay close attention to both the speaker and the audience. Teamwork can be demonstrated by affirming important points either with actual examples or a nod. Helping one another to keep the presentation on track also enhances success.

Another way to improve closing ratios is to tailor the presentation to a prospect's specific interests. Portfolio managers who address prospects' interests thoughtfully and completely, versus delivering a boilerplate presentation, make a powerful impression. Any information a prospect does provide needs to be confirmed before the presentation. Once confirmed as accurate, the information should be woven into the presentation. In addition to discussing competitive strengths and distinguishing characteristics, the portfolio manager must define the benefits to the prospect. Personalizing the benefits to a prospect's specific investment program is the most effective way to convey the quality of attention an account will receive after the prospect becomes a client.

The portfolio manager's skill at answering questions and addressing objections is as important as delivering an effective presentation. Some managers are better at the question/answer part of a presentation, while others eliminate themselves at this stage. The most common mistake is overanswering, and the worst is not to answer a question at all. Answers must be concise, honest, positive, and benefits-oriented. The most successful managers are those who consider likely questions and develop appropriate responses prior to the presentation. They devote as much time to preparing the questions and answers as they do the presentation.

Finally, to close the sale, the manager must gain the subjective vote. An investment organization may have a well-defined investment decision-making process, a highly qualified staff, and a good performance record, but the success of a presentation remains dependent on whether rapport is created between the prospect and the investment professionals. If the management firm's professionals share and exhibit spontaneity, confidence, enthusiasm, mutual respect, and reliance on one another, the potential is increased for the same feelings to be generated from the audience. Prospects must believe they can communicate with their manager and will enjoy meeting with him/her on a regular basis.

The presentations that win the most business have the following traits:

1. Understandable
   * Simplicity of language
   * Limited number of points covered

2. Credible
   * Show (proof statements) versus just tell
   * Confidence and enthusiasm
   * Honest and direct

3. Complete
   * All the information the prospect needs to make a decision
   * Never assume entire audience is equally knowledgeable

4. Powerful, positive language
   * Focus on what you are (versus what you are not)
   * Do not be defensive
   * Do not badmouth the competition

5. Excellent presentation skills
   * Body language = 60%; voice = 30%; words = 10%
   * Teamwork
   * Preparation and rehearsal
   * Dialogues versus monologues
   * Flexibility and responsiveness
   * Warmth, smiles

6. Cohesive, organized, appealing materials
   * High quality
   * Stand alone

7. Ability to respond to questions and objections well
   * Candid
   * Concise, positive, specific

Client Presentations

Client service and retention are priorities for most portfolio managers. Good performance alone does not safeguard client relationships. Firms experiencing even minor problems, such as a quarter or two of poor performance or professional turnover, often find their clients becoming their competitors' favorite hit list. Portfolio managers who do not meet with clients are the first to be fired in tough times.

Clients often dictate the frequency of formal meetings; however, portfolio managers should initiate informal communication with clients in good, neutral, and bad markets. Many clients enjoy tasteful entertainment periodically as well. Clients do not like to fire friends.

Once again, effective communication is the key to prosperous, long-term client relationships. One important goal for the portfolio manager in client presentations is to instill confidence and resell the reasons the manager's firm was hired. Acknowledging the client's investment objectives, showing how the investment team is fulfilling those objectives, and repeating the management firm's strengths is a worthwhile strategy in a client meeting.

Surprises must be avoided at all costs. The fastest way to lose a client is to let them first hear of significant news about their manager (e.g., departure of key professional; introduction of new investment product; change in investment style) through the grapevine. Plan sponsors prefer to work with people they can trust. Portfolio managers who address problems openly, honestly, and nondefensively have the highest credibility and the most patient clients.

A common complaint from plan sponsors is that their portfolio managers do not listen well. Managers frequently assure the prospect that they can meet the client's objectives before they are hired; then once in the door, they ignore objectives and deliver a standard product. One plan sponsor went so far as to call a meeting with all twenty-two of his investment managers in attendance, and asked them to write down the plan's investment objectives. The plan sponsor discovered that not one manager could describe the objectives and guidelines accurately. The portfolio manager who pays close attention to the client's objectives, guidelines, interests, and concerns can deliver superior, personalized service.

Managers who ignore client objectives and restrictions (e.g., against holding certain types of stock) find themselves replaced in a hurry.

Another avenue to improve service is defining the agenda for client meetings. The most responsive portfolio managers work closely with the client and, if applicable, the consultant to establish a meaningful agenda for client meetings. Meetings should not be just rote appearances covering performance, economic outlook, and holdings. The best meetings are dynamic and cover client objectives, issues currently facing clients, the investment product in context of the total plan, returns, and what to expect in the future. The portfolio manager is pro-active in suggesting topics, research and solutions.

Most portfolio managers walk clients through portfolio update booklets during the presentation. To show clients they are top priority, client presentation materials should be equal or better quality than marketing materials. The client materials should not be a standard cover letter with portfolio computer printout followed by twenty pages of economic charts. The materials should be user-friendly, appealing, highlight the information important to the client, and have a logical flow that supports the portfolio manager's presentation.

Client presentations also provide multiproduct management firms excellent cross-selling opportunities. Many plan sponsors prefer working with a limited number of managers. Managers that have done a good job for clients in one area can take advantage of the "halo" effect to introduce other products. After confirming with the client both the level of interest and time available, the portfolio manager can set up an introduction. Generally, it is most effective for portfolio managers to present alternative opportunities during a period of strong performance, at the end of a client meeting after covering the portfolio update.

Preparation, personalization, and appreciation for the client's business go a long way in building strong, long-term relationships. To safeguard client relationships, managers must exceed client expectations, if not in terms of performance, at least in terms of service.

Indirect Ways the Portfolio Manager Can Favorably Impact Presentations

The portfolio manager can help the sales professionals accelerate the sales process by being a team player. This means:

- being accessible to the marketing/sales professionals;

- respecting their contributions;

- communicating updates on portfolio action and strategy changes;

- providing "show" data (e.g., buy/sell examples);

- eliciting key objections heard in the marketplace;

- rehearsing prospect presentations, client meetings, and questions and answers; and

- being aware of prospect/client concerns.

Successful portfolio managers are never complacent or smug. They invite constructive criticism, seek ideas to improve their competitive positioning, and discover new ways to fulfill client and prospect needs. By assuming the client, prospect, or manager search consultant's point of view, a portfolio manager gains power that can be capitalized on in presentations.

The
Seven
Deadly
Sins

DOUGLAS B. REEVES

Senior Vice President,
Dain Bosworth, Inc.

Introduction

Billions of dollars in public pension funds are administered by boards of trustees who have little or no professional investment background. They do, however, represent the beneficiaries of the plans, the employees, and the taxpayers.

Whether or not the trustees have professional investment credentials, they are the people empowered to make decisions about the elaborate marketing plans presented by professional investment managers. Sometimes the trustees are guided in their deliberations by actuaries, consultants, accountants, and other advisors. Nevertheless, the final decision on the fate of investment management proposals rests with the collective judgement of the trustees.

This chapter provides some practical guidelines for investment management and marketing specialists who wish to communicate more effectively with institutional decision-makers. The thesis of this chapter is that trustees are neither country bumpkins nor sophisticated investment professionals—they are citizens doing their best to represent diverse constituencies and to make intelligent decisions. Investment managers and marketing specialists who fail to recognize the unique characteristics of public pension plan trustees as prospective clients will almost certainly fail in their attempt to win them as clients.

The Selection Process

Because of the large dollar amounts involved in public pension funds, interest in investment management contracts is intense. Although Wyoming is the least populous of the fifty states, its $1.2 billion retirement system attracted an extraordinary amount of interest when the trustees decided to seek new investment management. More than seven hundred managers requested the Request For Proposal. The investment committee, chaired by the author, reviewed all 260 of the submitted proposals. The investment committee was not atypical of groups found in public pension funds: a college professor of physics, a highway department official, an attorney, and a business person.

The sheer quantity of responses to a management search makes the written proposal the key ingredient to surviving the first cut of the selection process. A review of the marketing literature of most professional money managers reveals that they are, like the children of Lake Wobegon, all above average. There is, as a result, inherent subjectivity in the selection process. The distinctions in the rarified atmosphere of the best and brightest money managers are rarely made on the basis of a few tenths of a percentage point in the average return over the past ten years. In the case of the Wyoming retirement fund, for example, performance figures only narrowed the field from 260 to about fifty.

The final cut to the nine managers who were permitted to make oral presentations was substantially more subjective. There were many managers who offered apparently higher performance histories then the finalists, but nonquantitative elements of their proposals kept them out of the running.

Decision-making is collegial. It is neither possible nor useful to construct a decision framework to explain the mental process of every individual trustee. Managers rarely are chosen on a one-vote margin. Rather, a few managers rise to the top because they are able to appeal to a broad cross section of the committee or board. In the case under review, committee members ranked proposals A, B, or C in the first round of reviews. A manager receiving all A's was a clear choice to be a finalist—but each A might have been assigned for vastly different reasons.

Conversely, a C vote virtually assured no further consideration by the committee. Therefore, the strategy for survival of the first cut involves the *avoidance of critical errors*. Even though an error might be perceived as "critical" by only a single board member, the selection process involves the search for reasons to eliminate the contenders—not simply the identification of evident strengths.

The essential point for money managers and marketing specialists is this: a great track record simply is not enough to be competitive. Successful proposals feature not only a great track record, but are also able to appeal to different social and economic perspectives. Most importantly, the great proposals avoid offending any individual committee or board member to the point that the otherwise excellent proposal is doomed.

The Seven Deadly Sins

When this chapter was originally published, it quickly found its way into the hands of marketing training programs throughout the United States. Commentators ranged from "Wall Street Week" guests, to banking executives, to pension fund trustees, all of whom identified (sometimes with acute embarrassment) commission of the "sins" by themselves, their employees, or their competitors.

The reason for the emphasis on "sins" may appear to be unnecessarily negative. Why not instead emphasize the positive—what *should* investment managers and marketing specialists be doing? The answer is disappointingly simple: in the extraordinarily competitive atmosphere of modern investment management, one must presume that competitors are already doing nearly everything right. They have a good track record, they offer a depth of staff resources, their statements are accurate, their trading is quick and efficient, their reputation superb. The strategic advantage, therefore, is gained not merely by doing things right, but by avoidance of critical errors.

The other reason for the emphasis on "sins" is the collegial decision making nature of public trustees. When a single "No" vote can effectively veto a manager's selection, then simple affirmation is not sufficient—it is the avoidance of the vetoes which must be the hallmark of the successful proposal. Commission of one of the seven deadly sins does not mean that the manager submitting the proposal is a poor money manager—it simply indicates that the author of the proposal probably will not have very much money to manage. The sins explain why some very bright, sophisticated and well-managed investment firms are often eliminated from consideration for public fund management.

DEADLY SIN #1: FAILURE TO FOLLOW DIRECTIONS

The Woody Allen character who said, "Showing up is ninety percent of life" is not too far off. One might add, "Showing up at the right place, at the right time, and with the right information is ninety percent of a successful presentation." Trustees do not have infinite patience with people who cannot follow directions.

For example, if the trustees ask for a track record from January of 1983 through January of 1990, then serious respondents provide precisely those dates. It is the only way the trustees can make an "apples to apples" comparison. If the trustees ask for the number of people who are added to or subtracted from the ranks of investment managers, then a response which reads "there was no turnover of key personnel" is not sufficient. Bluntly put, if the investment manager submitting a proposal believes that the response to the questions asked by the trustees is none of the trustee's business, then the manager should save everyone some time and not participate in the selection process. In one instance of a very strong contender for final consideration in the Wyoming selection process, the trustees concluded that failure to be responsive to a relatively minor question indicated a lack of attention to detail, a vice that was not tolerable with $100 million of public money.

DEADLY SIN #2: IGNORING THE TRUSTEE'S INVESTMENT POLICIES

During recent years a number of public pension funds have adopted restrictive investment policies. Sometimes these policies are designed to meet social objectives, such as those that avoid investments in South Africa. In other instances, restrictive investment policies are designed to achieve the trustee's strategies with regard to risk limitation. Whatever the genesis of the restrictive investment policy, the proposal by an investment manager seeking to impress the trustees is not the appropriate forum in which to debate the merit of those policies. It is entirely possible that the trustees are not enamored of all of the restrictive policies any more than the investment manager. However, the prevailing policies reflect the consensus of a broad variety of political and social trends, and those policies must be respected.

The typical proposal blithely assures the reader that "we will have no difficulty conforming to your investment policy." In the Wyoming instance, however, fewer than twenty out of 260 proposals conveyed any impression of familiarity with the specific investment policies established by the trustees. More importantly, only a handful indicated the presence of specific mechanisms to monitor compliance with those policies. An astonishing number of proposals indicate a complete disregard of policies by extolling the virtues of investments that, although perhaps meritorious, are ineligible for inclusion in a particular public trust fund. One can argue that trustees ought to consider the use of such "sophisticated" investments as "high-yield" bonds, real estate, and venture capital, but the trustees of a number of public pension funds (who, it turns out, may have been wiser than the professional managers advocating these investments) have made policy decisions to avoid these investments. Managers who are not prepared to indicate explicit familiarity with prevailing restrictions and demonstrate mechanisms for dealing with these restrictions are more than likely to be eliminated by at least one board member who will find such an oversight unacceptable.

DEADLY SIN #3: OVERLOADING THE PROPOSAL WITH MARKETING TRIVIA

When a group of weary trustees are faced with the task of reviewing hundreds of proposals, the sheer weight of an individual proposal does not make a favorable impression. If, for example, the trustees asked for the biography of the pension manager assigned to their specific account, it is inappropriate to include the biographies of twenty colleagues in the same department. This conveys the unmistakable impression that the proposal was the product of mass production rather than the result of special attention given to this particular public fund. Pretentious pictures of the home office, action scenes of investment committee meetings, and the assorted studious faces of analysts are also of minimal assistance in making rational decisions. Simply put, the trustees should not have to play "hide and seek" in order to find the answers to the questions they have posed.

DEADLY SIN #4: CARELESSNESS

Modern word processors allow any firm to make a proposal which is professional in appearance. While the "bells and whistles" of adjustable fonts, type styles, type sizes, and professional graphics are not necessary for a persuasive proposal, it is essential that the proposal convey the impression of a professionally produced product rather than a high school term paper produced at the last minute.

Inept proofreading, poor reproduction, uneven margins, inconsistent literary style, and poor grammar are all factors which may seem unrelated to the realm of money management. When confronted with several excellent managers, however, trustees can easily use such care-lessness to easily eliminate a proposal that appeared to be written by someone who did not take the process very seriously. It is important to remember that the board of trustees of the pension fund may include several teach-ers of English, mathematics, and business.

DEADLY SIN #5: HARASSMENT

Public pension fund trustees typically give up a day or more each month to serve on the board. They rarely are paid and often are on the hot seat before legislative com-mittees, taxpayer groups, and employee associations. While this may not entitle them to sympathy, it should entitle them to respect. It is thus not helpful to the suc-cess of a prospective money manager to add to the trustee's burden by initiating calls from the would-be managers to the homes and offices of trustees. It is par-ticularly offensive when the citizen trustees are expected to return long-distance telephone calls at the expense of the trustee or their employers. Toll-free telephone num-bers are widely available and should be used.

The marketing specialists of money management firms are under enormous pressure to generate new ac-counts. What the trustee may regard as "harassment" may be simply "aggressive marketing" in the eyes of the director of marketing at the money management firm. To the marketing strategists in this field, the argument can be effectively made that the process of manager se-lection is a process of *elimination*—not merely a process of selection. *Every* irritation provides a reason for elimi-nation. In the Wyoming example, every single trustee commented on their displeasure with unsolicited sales calls.

Most firms are sufficiently wise to take a long-term view of their marketing strategy. Therefore, they should understand that calls to trustees from managers who are not selected are of limited value. While complaining, challenging, and berating of the trustees may be cathartic for the unsuccessful manager, they rarely create the sort of lasting impression that intelligent marketers would wish.

DEADLY SIN #6: MUDDY METHODOLOGY

The calculation of investment returns is not as difficult to understand as some managers would like to pretend. It is unwise to assume that because public trustees are not professional money managers, they are either stupid or totally unfamiliar with contemporary investment management techniques. One of the few light moments provided to trustees in the course of searching for a manager comes from the managers who devote the majority of their presentation to an elaboration of the reasons their management techniques and selection criteria are remarkably different from the universe of money managers. Such presentations overuse the words "unique" and "proprietary" and then provide a portfolio of securities which contains ninety percent of the securities owned by the managers from whom they, in theory, so widely diverge.

Whether the selection criteria is based on private market value, capitalized dividends, relative price-earnings ratios, or other factors, there ought to be a clearly stated investment policy that guides the investment manager. This policy should be articulated in a statement that is consistent between the marketing and analysis departments. The policy should be easily understood so that it can be discussed by lay trustees. Given several alternative proposals, all with great historical returns, trustees are most comfortable with the manager who can rationally explain how those returns were achieved. "Black boxes" and other contemporary alchemy of the investment world have little credibility.

The problem of muddy methodology is compounded when marketing staff people, rather than portfolio managers, attempt to explain it. As a matter of marketing strategy, the wise money managers recruit analysts who can speak, rather than sales people who know a little bit about analysis.

DEADLY SIN #7: "HELPFUL FRIENDS"

In the competitive world of financial services, there are an extraordinary number of people who wish to "help" money managers with the promise of influence and connections. Because money managers have witnessed many a decision which appeared to be based more on politics than rationality, the offer of help may be appealing. Money managers should, however, gain a much more healthy skepticism of those who would seek to promote the money manager in return for some unspecified consideration.

Like flies to the barn in summer, retail stockbrokers seek to affiliate with pension managers in order that the pension manager can claim some sort of "local" connection. This trend is disconcerting on several counts. First, it apparently presumes the trustees would be influenced by geography rather than competence. Second, the relationship between the local broker and the money manager is transparent. There is clearly no net gain to the local economy—simply a transfer payment from the remote money manager to a local opportunist. No analyst or support staff are going to move to the capital city because a local broker made a sale. Third, trustees are uncomfortable with any *quid pro quo* between manager and broker. The manager's responsibility is to get the best possible transaction execution in a competitive market. The appearance of a presumed payback to a local broker is at odds with this responsibility.

Local brokers may also subvert the marketing strategy of the money manager. While the money manager may scrupulously avoid the harassment of trustees referred to in Deadly Sin #5, the local "helpers" display little compunction when it comes to inappropriate contact with trustees.

A Better Way

Managers who win a competition usually are satisfied with the fairness and rationality of the process. The other ninety-nine percent are convinced that "there must be a better way." Perhaps the same is true of elections in a democratic society. But Plato's ideal in which the "men of gold" perpetuate their rule is not, for better or worse, characteristic of public pension fund management. Today's "men of gold" will be replaced by those who not only manage money well, but who also successfully communicate their capabilities to trustees. They will be given the opportunity to compete for this responsibility only if they can avoid commission of the deadly sins that eliminate them from this extremely competitive process.

An earlier version of this chapter appeared in *Pensions & Investments,* October 30, 1989.

INDEX